About the author

the Univers...y of L.......ick, I....and. ....e h.. p.......d
widely in the areas of glob.. p.....c.l ...n.my a... ..
particular in the areas of globalization, hegemony and
resistance. He is the author of *Hegemony, International
Political Economy and Post-Communist Russia* (2005),
and he co-edited *European Regionalism and the Left*
(with Gerry Strange, 2012), *Globlisation and the 'New'
Semi-Peripheries* (with Phoebe Moore, 2009) and *Critical Perspectives on International Political Economy* (with
Jason Abbott, 2002). He has published work on resistance and globalization in *Global Society*, *Globalizations*,
Capital and Class and *Third World Quarterly*, and has
also published in *International Politics*, *Review of International Studies* and *Journal of International Relations
and Development*. He is the current managing editor of
Capital and Class and is on the executive board of the
Conference of Socialist Economics.

RESISTANCE IN THE AGE OF AUSTERITY

NATIONALISM, THE FAILURE OF THE LEFT AND THE RETURN OF GOD

Owen Worth

Fernwood Publishing
HALIFAX | WINNIPEG

Zed Books
LONDON | NEW YORK

Resistance in the age of austerity: nationalism, the failure of the left and the return of God was first published in 2013.

Published in Canada by Fernwood Publishing, 32 Oceanvista Lane, Black Point, Nova Scotia, B0J 1B0 and 748 Broadway Avenue, Winnipeg, Manitoba, R3G 0X3

www.fernwoodpublishing.ca

Published in the rest of the world by Zed Books Ltd, 7 Cynthia Street, London N1 9JF, UK and Room 400, 175 Fifth Avenue, New York, NY 10010, USA

www.zedbooks.co.uk

FSC
www.fsc.org
MIX
Paper from
responsible sources
FSC® C013604

Set in FFKievit and Monotype Plantin by Ewan Smith, London
Index: ed.emery@thefreeuniversity.net
Cover design: www.rawshock.co.uk
Cover photo © iStock
Printed and bound by CPI Group (UK) Ltd, Croydon, CR0 4YY

Distributed in the USA exclusively by Palgrave Macmillan, a division of St Martin's Press, LLC, 175 Fifth Avenue, New York, NY 10010, USA

A catalogue record for this book is available from the British Library
Library of Congress Cataloging in Publication Data available

Library and Archives Canada Cataloguing in Publication

Worth, Owen, 1974-
    Resistance in the age of austerity : nationalism, the failure of the left and the return of God / Owen Worth.
Includes bibliographical references.
ISBN 978-1-55266-563-3
    1. Neoliberalism. 2. Financial crises--History--21st century.
3. Anti-globalization movement. 4. Right and left (Political science)--History--21st century. I. Title.
HB3717 2008.W67 2013   330.12'2   C2012-907761-5

ISBN 978 1 78032 336 7 hb (Zed Books)
ISBN 978 1 78032 335 0 pb (Zed Books)
ISBN 978 1 55266 563 3 (Fernwood Publishing)

CONTENTS

ACKNOWLEDGEMENTS

This book was a number of years in the making, but was largely written in the different locations of west Wales, Limerick and Perth, Australia, at the end of 2011 and beginning of 2012. I am grateful to Maura Adshead, at the time head of the Department of Politics and Public Administration at the University of Limerick, for giving me teaching relief for study leave at that time. I am also grateful to the faculty of Arts, Humanities and Social Sciences for seed funding in order to attend the World Social Forum in Nairobi in 2007. I would like to thank Gerry and Jackie Strange, Mark Beeson, Bruce Stone and the Politics and International Studies department at the University of Western Australia (UWA). I have benefited from feedback and discussions from several talks that I have given leading up to the writing of this book. I would like to thank Jason Abbott and those at the Center for Asian Democracy at the University of Louisville, Chris Farrands (as ever) and David Bailey for organizing an excellent panel at the ECPR conference in Reykjavik in August 2011. I have also benefited from excellent discussions with colleagues and former students and would in particular like to thank Luke Ashworth, Karen Buckley, Matt Merefield, Kyle Murray, Swati Parashar and Andy Shorten. On a personal level I would like to thank Perys, Rosa, Sam, Austen and family and my many colleagues, friends and family on both sides of the Atlantic and the Irish Sea.

INTRODUCTION: IN SEARCH OF A NEW PRINCE

He who wishes to be obeyed must know how to command
(Machiavelli, 1513)

The financial crisis that had engulfed the world by 2008 shook a whole genre of company directors, businessmen, economists, financial advisers and investors who believed that the market-generated global economy was structurally in safe hands. The fallout from the credit crisis and the subsequent banking collapses had an even greater knock-on effect on society in general as property mortgages that were encouraged and distributed at high rates became unsustainable. As production faltered and economies, at least in the developed world, began to slide into recession, the general social ills associated with depression economics began to surface.

In line with other periods of capitalist crisis in the past, its immediate aftermath saw a whole collection of soul-searching and analysis into how and why the system collapsed. This was perhaps demonstrated best when, as noted recently by David Harvey, Britain's Queen Elizabeth II questioned economists at the LSE as to why no one had seen the crisis coming. The response from economists was that they underestimated the importance of systemic risk within the workings of market economics as a whole (Harvey 2010: 235). Yet, for those who have located themselves outside the circle that worked, functioned and believed in the sustainability of the global economy, the crisis was not a surprise. For long, students of International Political Economy (IPE) have pointed to the unsustainability of the global economy. At the same time those who have been involved within, or have studied, the resurgence in protest movements that have emerged from civil society have aired their discontent at the ideological underpinnings of the global economy. The neoliberal principles that the global economy has been founded upon since the Thatcher–Reagan era of the 1980s have been much maligned by such criticisms, and it is these principles which have come under even greater scrutiny since the economic crisis.

Despite the underlying problems with neoliberalism being aired more freely since the financial crisis, there has been a reluctance to break away from its overall rhetoric and logic. One of the striking features of this crisis has been that an alternative form of economic governance has not been forthcoming. While the crash in 1929 paved the way for an era of Keynesian economics and the stagflation in the 1970s saw the emergence of neoliberal free market ideas, the current crisis has not really led to any fresh alternatives to neoliberalism. While there have been discussions on the reform of the economic system in the immediate aftermath of the crisis, a radical ideological overhaul of the way the global political economy is managed has never been seriously considered. Instead, there has been a commitment to ride out the crisis through the reduction of sovereign debt that increased in countries where banking bailouts have occurred, by reducing public funds to welfare. As a result the welfare state is being rolled back even more by the realities – if not the genuine ideologies – of neoliberalism.

The main purpose of this book is to look at whether or not, in light of the financial crisis, neoliberalism can sustain itself as the hegemonic ideology behind the governance of the global political economy. In particular it looks at potential challengers to the neoliberal system and questions whether such positions can muster a viable or coherent alternative project capable of altering the nature of the current world economic order. The decline of the USA, the rise of China and the more structured form of state capitalism that has been favoured by their stark economic growth might be one that could replace the neoliberal model, which has often been associated with American power (Beeson 2010). However, the realities of neoliberalism have seen multinational firms move their interests away from developed states to ones that offer cheaper labour costs, which have allowed for increased profitability for the larger multinational corporations. As a result, while the crisis has seen economies falter in the developed world, productivity and economic growth on a global level have continued to rise, with countries such as China and India, areas such as South America, the Middle East and Central Asia, all enjoying significant increases in economic growth in the last couple of years. Countries on the fringes of the European core, such as Turkey and the Baltic states, have benefited from the fallout in the financial heartland.

These circumstances all remind us of the observations made by Karl Marx when he looked at the processes and realities of free market capitalism in the nineteenth century. In his classic analysis of capital accumulation, Marx demonstrated that the capitalist system rested upon the acquisition of surplus value and the reliance on expanded profits through the reinvestment of this surplus (Marx 1976: 725–870). The international expansion of capital thus relies upon the continued pursuit by companies (or the class of the bourgeoisie) of profit maximization and new markets. As this allows for the globalization of free market capitalism, then during times of economic crisis in the heartland, greater productivity will emerge elsewhere. The twentieth century saw a reaction against this process as the prominence of both Keynes's work in criticizing the chaotic nature of free market capitalism (Keynes 2004), and the respective socialist projects (through both 'social democracy' and through state socialism or communism), put an end to the era of liberal capitalism. But the end of the Cold War and the effective ideological defeat of state socialism brought a new meaning to the idea of a global economy, as the effective opposition to unfettered capitalism appeared to have subsided. Over twenty years on, and with this post-Cold War form of global capitalism experiencing its first major systematic predicament, this book outlines the movements that are emerging from political and civil society that wish to construct alternatives to the status quo. A collection of movements that, as I intend to show, are far more diverse and less precise in their alternative visions than were the different forms of socialism in the twentieth century.

New Prince, modern Prince or postmodern Prince?

One of the much-commented-on criticisms of any opposition to neoliberalism is that while opponents are quick to illustrate the shortcomings of the contemporary system, they fail to outline viable alternatives to it. What they do not add is that such alternatives can be constructed by building a popular homogeneous movement that contains its own norms, laws and customs that are distinctly different to those inherent within the prevailing order. Writing from fascist captivity in the 1930s, the former communist leader Antonio Gramsci argued that for a socialist revolution to occur a transformation was required that would incorporate all facets of society so that a mindset would be formed that would differ fundamentally in its nature to that which preceded it. In this way, a transformation must occur in order for the common sense of everyday life to be altered in a manner that reflects the wider change in political economy (Gramsci 1971: 419–25).

Gramsci borrows from Niccolo Machiavelli's mythical 'Prince' in order to envisage such a change. Machiavelli gained notoriety for generations after the publication of *The Prince*, in which he stressed that a ruler should seek to strive for popularity as opposed to religious morality, if he wishes to enjoy stability during his reign. He describes the importance of the civil bond that the Prince must forge with the 'common-people' if he is to run a successful principality (Machiavelli 1984: 29–36). Gramsci pointed out that it was precisely this civil bond which was required for a socialist transformation to be successful. As Machiavelli was at pains to stress, leaders who rule without popularity rarely make successful sovereigns. Gramsci was equally keen to stress that a socialist project could not emerge like some scientific process in the manner that some Soviet theorists were arguing at the time. Instead the Prince appears, to quote directly from Gramsci, as 'a concrete phantasy which acts on a dispersed and shattered people to arouse and organise its shattered will' (Gramsci 1971: 126). Therefore Machiavelli's sixteenth-century Prince[1] is historicized and transformed into the vision of a potentially successful twentieth-century political movement by Gramsci four centuries later.

Gramsci's 'Modern Prince', as he defined it, was to represent the socialist movement as a whole. The real message behind *The Prince* was not that it appeared as a guide for rulers in city-states at the time, or, as many assumed, that it appeared as the first political treatise to legitimize the separation of state power from theology, but that it appeared as a metaphor of what is required in order for a specific political movement to mobilize itself towards a coherent and popular whole. In this way, Machiavelli's *The Prince* did represent a move against theology. Not as a sentiment that placed the autocratic reality of state sovereignty ahead of the morality of the Church, but as a reflection of the emergence of movements that would reinforce the state system's dominance over the Church. As the state system evolved, the bond between the ruler and the ruled within a bonded community would develop into the beginnings of nationalism.

Every era in contemporary world history can be defined by a moment when a Prince has emerged to construct a hegemonic order that has bonded together social classes behind an ideological cause. The Industrial Revolution saw the emergence of a liberal Prince that was encouraged by the work of Adam Smith and constructed through the emergence of the bourgeoisie. The social problems caused by the pursuit of liberal capitalism resulted in a succession of new Princes which sought for supremacy in the early part of the twentieth century (Cox 1987). It was within this context that Gramsci himself was writing. The post-war era found a variety of state socialist, social and Christian democratic Princes that were either influenced by the continuity of Marxism-Leninism or the mixed economic form of Western capitalism that was developed by Keynes. The neoliberal Prince that emerged as a response to the economic stagflation of the 1970s was one that was aided by the fall of the Soviet Union and carried by its popularity within the world's only remaining superpower.

Any attempt to challenge the basis of this current neoliberal order rests upon the ability to forge a new popular Prince capable of replacing its economic common sense with a set of alternative assumptions. Some have argued that a contemporary Prince must be constructed in a manner that moves firmly beyond national movements that have been shaped by the state system. Stephen Gill, for example, has argued that new forms of political agency are geared towards global transformation. Movements that have emerged from global civil society have aimed to establish a new Prince that is based upon universal values that seek to ensure 'human and intergenerational security on and for the planet, as well as democratic human development and human rights' (Gill 2000: 131–2). Gill argues that the twenty-first century needs a 'post-modern Prince in order for it to counter the failings of economic globalisations' (ibid.: 132–3). At the same time, others have argued that as the principles of free market economics were something that emerged from the political right, if the left wants to form a new Prince to challenge them, it needs to take this new political environment seriously and reorient its strategies (Sanbonmatsu 2003).

However, while this postmodern Prince may be one that those on the left might wish to build on, there are other Princes that have emerged that also seek to contest the contemporary system. These appear as reactions against the modernization that globalization and the global economy have produced. The increasingly prominent far right and far-right doctrines, highlighted most recently by the success of Marine Le Pen in the first round of the recent French presidential elections,[2] have attacked the effects that neoliberal globalization has had on the cultural and political tradition of the nation-state. Nationalism has re-emerged from the political fringes to attempt to construct its own Prince, based overwhelmingly on national mythologies and on the rejection of multiculturalism. Perhaps more noticeable has been the resurgence of religious resistance. This might have taken on real significance after the events of September 11th and the attack on the World Trade Center in New York as the public felt the full backlash of such resistance, but the significance of religion within global politics had been noted before that. The end of the Cold War saw an increase in religious movements as they began to fill the void that was left by the collapse of Marxism-Leninism, and to look to construct their own respective Princes based upon the primacy of religious interpretation.

The era of neoliberal globalization that we are currently living in has thus provided a number of potential Princes, which this study intends to show. While some might look to embrace a new form of politics that moves beyond the traditional boundaries that preceded it, many more seek to return to previously discovered ground in order to rekindle former myths and narratives.

The plan of the book

This book sets out to explore the longevity of free market capitalism by looking first at the actual content of contemporary neoliberalism before assessing the resistance that has emerged from it. The first chapter looks at how neoliberalism first surfaced after the crisis of the fallout from the collapse of the dollar system in the 1970s. However, as I argue, it did not emerge as a hegemonic project in its own right until the collapse of the Soviet Union and the end of the ideological confrontation between the East and the West. It was here that neoliberalism globalized and its general principles were taken up as norms within the governance of the global economy. The notion that the end of the Cold War marked some sort of watershed in historical terms is also discussed, as is the idea that neoliberalism, in its various guises, represents a new stage in the development of global capitalism.

From there, the book looks at the nature, form and conception of resistance in the global political economy. As such it reviews the number of frameworks that have been put forward so that resistance can be conceptualized and understood within the contemporary era. Moreover, the chapter shows that the triumph and euphoria that briefly occurred in the aftermath of the Cold War over the potential of a 'new world order' subsided into a discontent that emerged at different levels. It also illustrates how resistance has been formed according to contrasting sets of parameters, and so, while it has been diverse in nature, it has also been fragmented. Here, we see resistance stimulated by new forms of media and by new methods of organization, but these have also served to limit the extent of its coherence. As a result, the post-Cold War era of 'globalization' can be seen as one that has provided a great deal of opposition to the hegemonic project of neoliberalism, but little coherent alternative.

The subsequent chapters seek to explore what can be seen as the main hegemonic challengers to neoliberalism. Or, putting it another way, the general ideological traditions where a new Prince might emerge. The three traditions outlined might overlap in parts and might attract a great deal of criticism in the manner in which they have been categorized, but they do represent three general positions whereby an alternative hegemonic project might emerge. By locating them as coming from the right, the left and from 'above', or alternatively from a globalist, nationalist and religious orientation, we can at least illustrate the scope and content of such counter-hegemonic projects. As a result, the book seeks to look at how movements as diverse as Occupy, European far-right political parties and al-Qaeda have all emerged as forms of resistance to the contemporary global order.

While the bulk of this book aims to look at and evaluate these different forms of contestation, Chapter 6 turns to considering how neoliberalism has been defended in the light of the financial crisis. It shows that while these opposition movements would be expected to make inroads into the legitimacy of neoliberalism during this period of crisis, the proponents of neoliberalism have instead managed to go on the defensive by adopting austerity measures. Current political developments have seemed to suggest that the present neoliberal system can be salvaged by relying on austerity measures and cuts in public expenditure to provide a new incentive for the market to restimulate itself. Indeed, as I will show, new movements such as the Tea Party in the USA have arisen that provide a staunch defence of neoliberal principles and stress that it has been compromised by big government, excessive spending and raising taxation. In this way, to quote one recent commentator, 'neoliberalism is being used to address the faults of neoliberalism' (Macartney 2011).

The final chapter of this book looks at the wider implications of this defence of neoliberalism and whether or not austerity and crisis management can provide the stimulus for the neoliberal hegemony project to remain intact, or whether a future project will inevitably emerge to replace it. Particular attention is paid here to the emergence of the so-called BRIC (Brazil, Russia, India and China) economies (or BRICS, if we include South Africa, as in recent summits) and whether they can bring a different type of economic governance to the global economy. It then looks at what would be required for a more socially inclusive hegemonic system to challenge the current order by revisiting some of the Marxian and Gramscian literature of the 1980s and 1990s. In this way, the book seeks to address a number of themes. Not only does it highlight the vast array of resistance discourses that have emerged and discuss the reasons why to date these have not mounted a serious challenge in light of the present crisis, it also addresses some misinformed claims about the silence of social scientists in its aftermath. A recent article in the *Guardian* newspaper in the UK made the sweeping claim that while economics might have failed as a subject by not seeing the crisis coming, the other disciplines of social sciences have equally failed to conceptualize its fallout or look at alternatives (Chakrabortty 2012). As this study shows, it is not the lack of interest in the crisis which has blighted academic studies in recent years, but the failure of those in practical politics to realize the scope of this work.

1 | THE END OF HISTORY?

Men believe in the truth of that which is plainly strongly believed
(Friedrich Nietzsche, *Human, All Too Human*)

In 1989 Francis Fukuyama, reflecting upon the events that were
unfolding in eastern Europe, proclaimed in a conservative-leaning
US-based journal that 'history' was ending (Fukuyama 1989). Civilization was effectively reaching the end of its centuries-old struggle,
with freedom and liberal democracy, propelled by the free market,
emerging as the victors. Following the same observations that had
prompted Hayek and Von Mises to make respective assertions that the
free market remained society's best yardstick for ensuring individual
liberty and freedom (Hayek 2001 [1944]; Von Mises 1949), Fukuyama
suggested that humanity had dialectically reached the same conclusion.
While by no means perfect, it was strong enough to see off respective
state-managed alternatives of all guises. Yet the imperfections of liberal
democracy were to become evident as soon as the transition from a
bipolar world to a post-Cold War world began.

What emerged in the 1990s, in the aftermath of the fall of communism, was a number of developments that quickly added to the
disenchantment with the new post-Cold War era. The painful transition that former socialist countries faced when embracing the market
were coupled with a renewal of ethnic tensions that produced new
instabilities and new sources of resistance. Likewise, the promise of a
'New World Order' by George Bush Sr, whereby a new post-Cold War
environment would be pursued by all states, was also not realized. Indeed, many strategic 'realists', uneasy that their Cold War assumptions
were now being undermined, responded by insisting that the stability
of the bipolarity that marked the Cold War would be replaced by a
far more dangerous multipolar environment (Mearsheimer 1990; Waltz
1993). Certainly, the euphoria surrounding the post-Cold War moment
was short lived, and debates almost immediately began to emerge over
the future configuration of world politics. If in the 1990s US power
seemed to favour an increased use of international organizations within

international affairs, then the events of September 11th 2001 changed this tendency. The fallout from 9/11 saw a neoconservative turn in US foreign policy, whereby the administration under George W. Bush turned to military force without the support of the United Nations. The reaction to the campaigns in Afghanistan and Iraq has added to the discontentment with any US-inspired form of political project and further complicated any vision of universal liberal democracy.

Yet it has been the wider project of 'neoliberal' globalization which has best defined the character of the post-Cold War era. Emerging out of the Thatcher–Reagan doctrines of the 1980s, neoliberalism became the dominant model for economic development in the 1990s. The freeing up of markets from state constraints, combined with technological advances, allowed for a globalization of the economy to an extent not witnessed before. While debates have been aired over how far this process has actually gone and how far the global market has actually succeeded as a totalizing force in world politics (Hirst and Thompson 1996), the period succeeding the end of the Cold War can be seen as one where free market capitalism has been unchallenged as a form of economic global governance. The main purpose of this first chapter is to illustrate how neoliberalism emerged as a hegemonic project and how its negative effects have been such that the triumphalism that accompanied claims that history had ended appeared unfounded.

Neoliberalism: an ideology and a practice

While the realities of neoliberalism did not emerge until the 1980s in the financial heartlands of the world, its roots date back in theory to wartime Britain and in practice to military dictatorships in South America in the 1970s. While the Austrian School of Economics had kept the fire of classical economics burning, it was Friedrich von Hayek's *Road to Serfdom* that would be regarded as the bible for liberal radicals during the post-war era of Keynesian-dominated economics. It would then – more importantly – appear as a guidebook for practitioners and politicians who actively endorsed the principles of the neoliberal new right.

The main message within the *The Road to Serfdom* was a simple one: namely that no matter how well intentioned it is, state intervention in economy is ultimately an erosion of liberty (Hayek 2001 [1944]: . Any form of collectivism and state planning ultimately leads to a bigger state that, once enlarged, seeks greater authoritarian power. As such, social forms of centralization rely upon forms of 'restraint and servitude' in order to succeed and erode key human advances such as liberty and democracy (ibid.: 24–31). More prominently at the time, it also argued that the origins of fascism were rooted not in a crisis of capitalism but in the increased conviction that intervention and planning would stabilize the capitalist system. This led to an increased momentum for a socialist alternative to capitalism, which, for Hayek, developed in different forms. As Italian fascism (through the Italian Socialist Party), Nazism (from National Socialism) and communism (through Marxism-Leninism) all emerged from different forms of socialist planning and all relied upon authoritarian measures, then Western parliamentary versions would have a similar fate (ibid.: 171–207).

At the time the book had mixed reviews. Although it was later to be used as an attack on the very fabric of Keynesian economics, Keynes himself liked it, but was of the opinion that it served no practical relevance. In the non-Soviet post-war world, the book was interpreted differently. In the USA, its popularity coincided with the emergence of the Cold War, and it sat suitably within a growing list of anti-Soviet literature. In Britain, however, the book met with opposition in a wave of support for the democratic socialism that accompanied the election success of the Labour Party. Highly accessible and confrontational, Hayek's magnum opus was to find new popularity in the 1970s when, in the aftermath of the collapse of the Bretton Woods system of economic regulation, the free market ideals returned. The decade became synonymous with stagflation and with the debt states were amassing in order to cover their respective fiscal cycles. While Hayek's wisdom might have appealed philosophically as a fresh challenge to the Keynesian status quo, a new body of economists that became known as the 'Chicago School' were setting out how such a challenge might be realized. By adopting a monetarist approach to the economy, states could control the growth rate of the money supply, leading to a reduction in inflation. Associated primarily with the work of Milton Friedman, the leading light of the Chicago School, monetarism was to become prominent in the elections of both Reagan and Thatcher and in the financial management of Chancellor Kohl in Germany. Yet it was in Argentina and more prominently in Chile, that the new doctrines were initially tested.

The Chilean coup in 1973 removed the democratically elected leader, Salvador Allende, and a military dictatorship, under the leadership of General Augusto Pinochet, took its place. Under his guidance, Chile went through a transformation of its economy that included wide-scale privatization, monetary restraint, the opening up of the economy to foreign ownership and investment and tax reforms. In addition a number of Chilean Chicago-educated economists under the guidance of Friedman were charged with the management of this process. Chile's role as the laboratory of the neoliberal experiment was such that Hayek himself visited the country many times, stating that he preferred a 'liberal dictatorship to a democratic government lacking liberalism' (Grandin 2006: 171). Thus, while the Hayekian ontology rested upon the correlation between the reduction of state involvement in the economy and liberty, the irony was that only through state oppression and the suppression of popular democracy could the concentrated form of neoliberalism succeed. The experience in Chile was to spread to neighbouring Argentina, which, through the same form of military dictatorship, embarked upon a similar economic project, although it never reached the same heights and was compromised by populist intervention later in the decade.

Yet it was the experience in Chile which inspired many new right-wing campaigners in the USA and the UK and set the foundations for the spread of neoliberalism in the developed world. While the Thatcher–Reagan governments in the 1980s might be heralded as the main starting point for neoliberal hegemony, both experienced very different transformations. In the case of the USA, Reaganomics became more of a mind-set than a radical transformation. Through a network of academics, think tanks and business representations that were driven by the ontology of the Chicago School, the Reagan administration brought in a mentality that favoured tax cuts and a drastic reduction in 'big' government (Harvey 2005; Peck 2010). In the UK, a far greater revolution occurred, as labour union power was drastically reduced, wholesale privatization of state-owned utilities occurred and public sector pay was curtailed. This propelled a period of economic growth by the end of the decade, but at a cost to wider society. The process of deindustrialization occurred as industry was faced with a new era of market competition as businesses looked for cheaper imports overseas. This led to mass-scale urban degeneration. In terms of income distribution, the UK went from being one of the most egalitarian states in western Europe to one of the most unequal (Prasad 2006). In the decades that followed, inequality in the USA would also substantially increase as successive administrations continued the culture of tax cuts and regulations were consistently rolled back in the workplace.

While there had been a significant shift in the ideological management of the economies in the USA and the UK, the practical reality was different. Reaganomics was praised for drastically reducing inflation, rekindling economic growth in the USA and restoring individual liberties through tax cuts. However, rather than reducing spending substantially, which supply-side economists had set out to do, the Reagan administration only nominally reduced the growth rate of federal spending and actually averaged a higher rate in terms of percentage of GDP than the mean rate in the last three decades of the twentieth century. This was partly due to the increase in the defence budget that was eventually to become known as the 'second Cold War' and would result in a costly return to the arms race. Similarly, in the UK, the effects of the monetarist policies of Thatcher's first term, combined with her own conflict in the Falklands (ironically against one of the few states that had experimented with neoliberalism), reduced any potential for growth. Indeed, as the UK found, the control of monetary supply can be achieved only if the economy is structurally sound. The increase in unemployment and failure to instigate growth in the 1980s meant that a stringent monetary plan would be difficult in an advanced democracy where economic failure would be punished by the electorate.

What emerged as a consequence of the failure to stem state spending was an increase in debt. This was particularly noticeable in the USA, where tax cuts meant that borrowing was required by the government in order to cover fiscal demands. Yet it was the use of speculation and of credit which became embedded within the financial centres of New York and London and was to become a common component of everyday neoliberal life. As Andrew Gamble illustrates, tax cuts may have been used to stimulate the economy, but the encouragement of credit and borrowing in both the public and private sectors as well as to citizens and individuals led to the autonomous growth of financial institutions and banks and to the growth of the credit bubble (Gamble 2009: 15–16). It was the concentration on this growth incentive which was to characterize the neoliberal strategy and was to allow markets, financial institutions and companies to globalize.

The globalization of neoliberalism

If neoliberalism was an ideology that emerged from an economic crisis and was popularized through respective 1980s governments in the USA and the UK, then its global influence was ensured through institutional advancement and through was has been called the 'internationalisation of the state' (Picciotto 1991; Cox 1987). The former has been seen in incentives provided by institutions such as the World Bank and the International Monetary Fund (IMF) as an attempt to solve the problem of debt repayments in predominantly developing countries. As the 1970s became a decade of economic crisis in the advanced states, it also provided emerging independent nations with the first opportunity to control specific international market commodities. The oil crisis in 1973 showed how developing countries could use the power of raw materials for their own ends. As a result many states pursued extensive investment programmes in order to develop potential natural reserves, using high-interest loans. By the 1980s, states were amassing debt and repayment issues to an extent that the World Bank devised a series of measures that would include conditional aid. The plan initiated in 1989 sought to implement neoliberal policies in indebted countries through the use of structural adjustment programmes. It became known rather notoriously as the 'Washington Consensus'.

In brief the Washington Consensus aimed to transform economies by ensuring that states maintained fiscal policy discipline; reforming tax regimes to attract investment, setting competitive interest rates and exchange rates to attract investors, introducing trade liberalization and internal tariff reduction, privatization and deregulation, and the liberalization of inward foreign direct investment (FDI) (Williamson 1989). As a result, states have opened up their economies in order to comply with institutional pressures and have sought to privatize many basic public provisions in order to comply with such measures. The results of the Washington Consensus have been numerous. First, by virtue of its opening up several developing and emerging economies, many companies have been able to use the favourable conditions for their own benefit. Multinational corporations have long used labour and raw materials in less-developed states to maximize profits, but the opening up of markets has allowed corporations greater autonomy and influence in certain areas as states have become dependent upon them as domestic employers. Secondly, it contributed towards what is commonly referred to as the global division of labour. In theory, such a division traditionally appealed to Ricardian idealists as a condition in which concepts such as comparative advantage can be realized. Yet the reality has been one in which regions are being predominantly split into certain categorizations of production. The increase in the influence of foreign investment and multinational companies has consolidated this trend. Perhaps more important has been that the Washington Consensus has enabled the utilization of international economic governance based upon neoliberal principles. As in the cases of Chile and Argentina above, it was not endorsed by democratic mandate but by a supranational governmental body demanding certain objectives and economic targets.

If the Washington Consensus sought to extend the workings of the neoliberal project to the developing world then the end of the Cold War provided an opportunity to not just extend the practice to the post-communist world but also to put pressure on the sustainability of alternative models of capitalism. In this respect, Fukuyama and his fellow travellers were correct to bask in the victory of liberal capitalism in the aftermath of the Cold War. For, while the Soviet model of state socialism was unable to compete with Western capitalism, the emerging model of free market capitalism was seen to be the most viable solution to the ideological debate that had resounded since the Second World War. The argument was that, as Soviet-style socialism failed, then so had the Western version of welfare socialism. Or, to put it more strongly, as Ralf Dahrendorf did: socialism in all of its variants was dead (Dahrendorf 1990: 40). More importantly, this demise took away the threat of the 'red peril' of communism that had concerned conservative politics so much since 1945. With the socialist alternative seemingly on the retreat, the social concessions that previous centre-right thinking believed were needed to stave off the threat of communism were no longer required. One of the big pushes in western Europe during the Keynesian era was that not only should the economy be regulated to avoid potential instabilities, but that social inequality between the classes also needed to be reduced. The Keynesian compromise suited both the left and the right at the time, since, just as the left could claim that it allowed for measures that could be interpreted as a form of parliamentary socialism, so the right accepted Keynes's proclamation that social intervention in the economy was required to 'save capitalism' from itself and from potential 'draconian' alternatives. Yet in the aftermath of the demise of the Soviet Union such requirements were no longer necessary, especially as post-communist states themselves seemed prepared to fully embrace market ideology.

Eastern Europe's embrace of neoliberalism was evident in the years that followed 1989 as countries such as Poland, Hungary and the newly formed states of the Czech Republic and Slovakia went through market-based transformations. Here different degrees of economic therapy – designed to remove price controls, withdraw state subsidization and prompt privatization over a short space of time, as well as tax reforms and trade liberalization – occurred with contrasting effects (Dale 2011). Yet it was in Russia that the most negative effects seemed to occur. Backed by a keen American government, a collection of economists in US-based institutions and policy-makers in the World Bank and IMF set out to advise Russia on the form of its market transformation. Aping the Chilean practitioners who were trained by prominent members of the Chicago School, similar ideological treatment was given to Russian officials (Cohen 2000). The resulting shock therapy in the early months of 1992 became unmanageable, with price liberalization leaving the country with an influx of goods and increased prices that it was unable to control. Added to this was the fact that the hierarchal bureaucratic system of governance that was apparent within the Soviet Union – known collectively as the *nomenklatura* system – remained in place. As a result, when Russia's privatization process was set in motion in the following years, prominent members of the *nomenklatura* could use their positions to exploit the process. The result was that wealth became concentrated around an elite, which was to make the economy unproductive and prone to collapse. By the end of the century Russia's influx of FDI had dried up to the extent that a state-led move to break up Russia's oligarchic structure was initiated by new president Vladimir Putin in order to make the Russian economy more competitive.

The fact that, by the turn of the century, a country such as Russia had put such emphasis on competitiveness within the international economy offers some explanation of how far the importance of interaction with economic globalization has become to states. In order to pursue economic productivity many states in the developed world have sought to restructure their internal dynamics in order to attract overseas investment. The process of internationalizing a state's outlook in order to achieve economic growth has been another indication that the global market has taken on new significance in terms of how national economies are run. Thus one of the consequences of neoliberalism has been that states have sought to opt for strategies that at one level might seek to retain national infrastructures, but on another to make them competitive and highly compatible with the global economy (Cerny 1997). For example, the Nordic model of economic growth prided itself on an extensive welfare system and a high level of government spending. Faced with the reality of attracting foreign investment, the Nordic model moved to reduce corporation tax, allowing Scandinavian countries to be seen as having some of the world's most open economies, while retaining their high levels of income tax at home.[1]

Other countries sought to embed themselves more openly in the global economy in order to encourage international investment. For example, both Iceland and Ireland experienced 'economic miracles' when they sought to offer companies and investors unique services or skills that other states were more reluctant to do. Both offered low corporation tax and substantial tax breaks for multinational companies to relocate to their respective countries, and also provided the necessary labour skills by investing heavily in the education sector. Iceland also offered financial services with high interest rates that attracted overseas investment. Both were held up as being great models of economic innovation at the time and were also used as examples of successful neoliberal development by economic think tanks and business spokesmen who in turn used these models of internationalism as suggested directions for governments and politicians in other countries. As a result, eastern European states that have been newly subsumed into the European Union, such as the Baltic states and Slovenia, have similarly concentrated on providing an economic environment in which multinational firms might invest. Such a strategy places great reliance upon maintaining levels of FDI and risks great derogatory effects if capital flight (whereby investment is either withdrawn or moved to another state or region, leading to a sudden slump in productivity) should occur. In addition, by opening up an economy to international forces, states become prone to global upturns/downturns. This has been seen especially with the global economic crisis, where open economies, and in particular small states such as Ireland and Iceland that have 'internationalized' their economies, have suffered significantly. Therefore, states that were quick to adapt their national economic strategies to the emerging global market were often rewarded by record growth during the boom and the financial crisis has hit them just as hard.

Competing economic models have suffered in the wake of the dominance of the Anglo-Saxon or neoliberal model of development since the 1990s. This has especially been seen in Europe, where the continental model of capitalism has had great constraints placed upon it. Favoured in Germany, France and in the Benelux countries, the continental model advocates greater regulation of industry and job protection. It has also traditionally levied a relatively high level of corporation tax. Towards the end of the Cold War a wider, more inclusive version of the continental model was envisaged by Jacques Delors in the form of a social Europe (Delors 1988), and in the early years of the 1990s this appeared as Delors' own version of an 'end of history'. Yet, as neoliberal prominence began to spread, states such as Germany and France began to suffer economic stagnation as their labour markets became less flexible than other emerging markets in Europe. At the same time, the EU itself was emerging as an institutional forum where the idea of a more social Europe was in constant conflict with one that favoured a more open, neoliberal Europe (Strange and Worth 2012). Germany itself lowered its rate of corporation tax in line with others, in this way compromising its own form of development in order to engage with the increasing neoliberal norm. As outlined above, this follows similar compromises made to other alternative models, such as the Nordic model, yet it could be argued that the contradictions that have been apparent within the recent neoliberal transformation of the Nordic model are perhaps not as stark as those that have occurred with the continental model.

Another factor that accounted for the supremacy of neoliberalism was the decline of the neo-mercantilist alternative in East Asia. While this region was for years seen as the manufacturing success story of the developing world, the Asian economic crisis of 1997 was understood as being a failure of the uncompetitive and stagnant forms of governance that were unable to come to terms with the new demands of the global market (Harvey 2005: 96–7). As had been the case with previous economic downturns, the IMF's prescription for a cure was neoliberal restructuring. Here, capital controls were freed up and loans were provided on condition that specific liberalization targets were met, with the intention of breaking the forms of crony capitalism and protection that had previously been successful during the tiger years and fully integrating these economies into the neoliberal global economy.

To a degree, one of the emergent winners of the moves taken in light of the Asian financial crisis was China. Originally inferior as a global player to the Asian tigers, China responded to the end of the Cold War by establishing itself as a source of cheap and skilled labour. China's huge growth and significance on the international stage have had some interesting and potentially paradoxical features. On one level, China has, as David Harvey is quick to point out, developed a form of neoliberalism with what he calls 'Chinese Characteristics' (ibid.: 120–51). As China has emerged (along with India) as a manufacturing hub of the global economy, its state-managed approach to neoliberalism has brought with it less baggage than in other states owing to the absence of independent labour representation. In addition, the Chinese Communist Party has legitimized the engagement of neoliberal principles as being a key stage within the socialist mode of development (Shirk 2004). The success of the Chinese economy has potentially untold consequences for future developments. As we have learnt so far, those unrestricted by forms of participatory democracy have been more successful in implementing neoliberal policy, and it has been through the authoritarian structure of the state that China has been able to make huge strides into the global economy. However, this provides a potential Achilles heel for the sustained future of the neoliberal project. Owing to its success, China has increasingly been seen to be on a collision course with the USA in terms of its growing influence and in the direction that the global economy might go. At present, one third of US debt that is held by foreign states is owned by China. While this might demonstrate greater cooperation by leading states in order to attempt to preserve a neoliberal stability, it also demonstrates the role China can play and the power it can wield within the international system, and this might clash with the form and content of the future global economy. This leads us ultimately to the question of what drives neoliberalism and whether or not it is dependent upon the prominence of one specific state.

Neoliberal hegemony

One way of understanding how the neoliberal agenda has gained prominence as the working model for international political economy is through the notion of hegemony. Hegemony has long been used in the discipline of International Political Economy (IPE) to understand a form of dominance that one state has over the overall international system. Hegemonic Stability Theory, for example, has argued that periods of history where one state has appeared dominant have coincided with periods of stability as that state leads a system towards productivity (Kindleberger 1981). The collapse of the Bretton Woods and dollar system that marked post-war international economics left many at the time questioning whether the USA was in decline (Keohane 1984). Yet it was during this decline that the neoliberal revolution took off, and the end of the Cold War saw the USA not as the leader in decline, but as the only superpower remaining in the world. Following this logic, one might suggest that the spread of neoliberalism is a direct result of reconstituted US hegemony.

Yet the term hegemony is one that is used in different ways and for different purposes. While some argue that the international spread of neoliberalism should be identified as a form of imperialism (see, for example, Callinicos 2009), many have increasingly utilized Antonio Gramsci's concept of hegemony in order to understand its class dynamics. For Gramsci, the term hegemony referred to the process whereby the dominant class in society reaches a harmonious relationship with the lower or 'subaltern' classes by virtue of which certain norms and conditions are embedded. Writing from a fascist prison in Italy in the 1920s and 1930s, Gramsci, a prominent leader in the Italian Communist Party, questioned why factory workers in Italy continued to support the government, despite being economically disadvantaged by the system. Gramsci wrote a selection of prison notebooks in which he discussed how a hegemonic relationship is forged. He paid specific attention to Italian civil society and to the role of institutions such as the Catholic Church in order to understand how ideas and 'common sense' are forged in society.[2]

The main purpose behind Gramsci's interest in understanding hegemony was that he believed a socialist alternative to capitalism would have to be one which contained a firm hegemonic component. Thus he wanted to understand the dynamics of how a capitalist system is maintained in order to envisage and construct ways it could be contested. This is an area which I shall return to in the next chapter when considering the different forms of contestation. Here, however, it needs to be demonstrated how these forms of social and cultural neoliberal ideas have been moulded into common sense and everyday life. They can often be seen at the political as well as at the sociocultural level and differ from country to country and region to region in the manner in which they are articulated. As we have seen, the neoliberal project may have started in full force in the USA and the UK during the 1980s, but the construction of its content occurred in different ways and through very different mediums.

The reduction in union power and 'big' government has been central to restructuring the common sense of politics and political culture. While the labour movement has contested the move to reduce its influence, as in the coalfields of northern England and South Wales and the public sector strikes in France through to the openly confrontational strikes for union recognition and against privatization in South Korea and Argentina respectively, these have not brought an end to the conviction that the era of collective bargaining on the factory floor is no longer viable in light of the competitive nature of the global economy. Popular incentives such as low income tax have been used as ways of gaining consent, especially if presented as an extension of individual liberty. Yet, as mentioned with the cases of the Nordic states, high income tax and high state spending can be retained. Instead, politically, states have been bounded by the principle that integration into the global market is a primary necessity and one that must be prioritized in political life.

Yet the main form of political common sense that has emerged through neoliberalism has been the affirmation that the market is an untouchable force that must be worked with as opposed to something that can be controlled. The market mentality that has emerged within politics is not something that is in any way novel. Here similarities can be made with what the political economist Karl Polanyi described as the 'commodity fetishism' of the nineteenth century. In his study of classical British liberal society, the self-regulated market became such that all forms of political life were subordinated by it. As a result all laws and norms become open to the market and are commodified (Polanyi 2001 [1944]: 60–2). It has been this general mind-set that has come to dominate the fabric of politics in the twenty-first century. Social democratic parties have largely failed to contest or indeed construct any meaningful alternative to this mind-set. This can especially be seen with compromises such as the 'third way' that were fashionable in parts of Europe in the late 1990s and early parts of the twenty-first century. Conceived originally in a short and approachable textbook by the prominent sociologist Anthony Giddens, 'third way' ideology argues against both social democratic economic intervention and laissez-faire economics and instead favours a system where the public and private sectors can steer the market in a progressive direction. Thus, as opposed to the more hard-line ideology of the 1970s and 1980s, the third way sees the market and the private sector as an avenue that can lead to greater inclusivity and welfare provision (Giddens 1998: 101–18). Giddens's book became highly influential, not just in Europe but also in places such as South America and Asia post-crisis, where the belief that globalization and the global economy could be used as a catalyst for development gained purchase with centre-left figures such as Cardoso in Brazil (Cardoso 2001).

Technically, the third way differed from the neoliberal ideology of Thatcher–Reagan, yet it largely amounted to the same commitment to market reform and to the reduced role of the state in the economy. Indeed, in reality, one could argue that this form of neoliberalism with a human face actually represents a truer depiction of a Hayekian vision of politics, as the state plays a more active role in steering the market towards a more feasible outcome. It was this reality which was played out during the Clinton administration in the USA, New Labour in the UK and within emerging regional bodies such as the European Union as neoliberalism remained in the ascendancy. Centre-right organizations were still able to attack such approaches for raising state spending in order to facilitate a more humanistic endeavour. Indeed, as we shall see in Chapter 6, one of the political criticisms to emerge in light of the global economic crisis was that states have been spending too much and that government waste on failed initiatives has added to the debt burden.

Political common sense has been complemented by the culture of individualism and consumerism. The emphasis on entrepreneurship, on investment and on participation in the stock and property market has been one that many employers have encouraged, particularly in the more open economies, while successful and powerful entrepreneurs have been widely heralded as role models. Indeed, one of the features of the reconstruction of the centre-left has been its attraction to self-made businessmen and philanthropists such as Bill Gates, Alan Sugar and George Soros, who have been keen to stress the social potential and inclusivity of market innovation. This has been particularly the case for development, where a commitment to using business initiatives to invigorate economies and aid the process of poverty alleviation has been stressed by economists such as Jeffrey Sachs. Here the belief is that the market has not been allowed to be used to its full potential as factors such as debt repayment and corruption have got in its way. Accordingly, used correctly, multinationals and technological innovation can be employed in a manner that can allow states to develop socially and to be economically sustainable (Sachs 2005). This again adds fuel to the common-sense idea that the market can solve all problems.

If the spirit of entrepreneurship has provided a moral dimension to neoliberalism, then the growth of consumerism has certainly led to its cultural development. The burgeoning of product-based multi-national companies and the growth of the 'brand' or the 'logo' have vastly contributed to neoliberalism's sustainability. Cultural studies analysts have questioned whether this move has been one of cultural imperialism or Americanism, whereby products and consumer goods have emerged and are reproduced in the image of Western culture, or whether the spread of such goods could be compatible with local cultures and customs and developed in a hybrid form (Nederveen-Pieterse 2004). This brings up the familiar debate concerning the role of multinational companies and the way that their goods are consumed, and the argument over whether a company is appearing as a dominator or as a facilitator of a product that is in local demand. It remains the case, however, that the globalization of consumerism has facilitated an important form of cultural agency in the success of neoliberalism as the popularity of and demand for international brands strengthen the relationship of consent between classes.

The complex relationships between the facilitators and the con-senters of hegemony ultimately bring us back to a wider question of how hegemony is facilitated. One of the many debates that has surrounded the application of Gramsci's concept of hegemony to neoliberalism is whether it can appear as a set of separate national projects or as a single international or global hegemonic project (Germain and Kenny 1998; Worth 2008). The point here, however, is that while neoliberalism has been articulated through different mediums and at different levels, it has nevertheless appeared as the overriding ideology behind the global economy. Many have argued that the starting point for this remains US power and that neoliberal ideology relies largely on the fabric of the US state for its expansion (Rupert 2009, for an excellent demonstration of this). Others have suggested that a transnational capitalist class has been formed across national boundaries and that neoliberalism has been constructed internationally through the actions of these elites (see Van der Pijl 1998 for the best historical study of this). Yet while the actions of those at the top of the hierarchy might provide us with the basis for neoliberal mobilization, the manufacturer of its consent rests with what Gramsci terms the 'traditional' and 'organic' intellectuals.

Intellectuals play a key role in the fashioning of hegemony, and are, to quote Gramsci 'the dominant group's "deputies" exercising the subaltern functions of social hegemony and political government' (Gramsci 1971: 12). The traditional intellectuals are those that hold formal positions, such as politicians, teachers, priests and, in the contemporary era, entrepreneurs, business elites, etc. Organic intellectuals, however, are those that appear as leaders of specific social groups and can appear on every level. For example, workers' representatives can be considered organic intellectuals as they function as important cogs in the running of the workplace. In the functioning of hegemony, they can be seen as anyone that communicates and reiterates the dominant ideology's overriding common sense. Gramsci was particularly keen on looking at the role that intellectuals play in language, folklore, religion and popular culture. In terms of contemporary neoliberalism, organic intellectuals have used popular culture through the mediums of communication and through media conglomerations that have become central in strengthening its consent. For example, the birth of the tabloid newspaper culture and the rise of multinational media enterprises have played significant roles in the reinforcement of the free market (Herman and McChesney 1997). This has been seen in both the manner in which news and political content are reported and their content, as well as in the way in which consumerism and consumer products are promoted. Notable state-owned companies such as the BBC have had to compete with commercial giants such as CNN and Fox News in their media production. Likewise, similar forms of media outlets have integrated narratives of national and historical folklore so that they appear compatible with the workings of contemporary capitalism. For example, companies such as Murdoch's News Corporation have successfully managed to repackage their products across a variety of different continents by responding to specific national and regional cultural differences. In this manner national and non-Western cultures that have often been rooted in anti-Western practices have reframed such narratives in a manner that fits in with the workings of global capitalism.

The gaining of consent in civil society may have provided the ingredients for neoliberalism's growth and success, but the very manner in which it is assembled also provides the very fabric for its resistance. For, as we have seen, while modern forms of communication can secure forms of consent, they can also contest them. As we shall see in the subsequent chapters, forms of new media and technological advances have been used to further the process of neoliberalism, and organic intellectuals and social groups have emerged to contest the very basis of neoliberal principles. For example, inventions such as the Internet have allowed space where both consolidation and contestation can occur. Its very existence and influence have been dependent upon open economies and the free market, yet the advent of cyberspace has allowed dissent to flourish in abundance. The ability for groups to emerge and organize dissent through these new media might have been something that abated within years of the end of the Cold War, but it became permanent in the light of the attacks on the World Trade Center on September 11th 2001.

After the second 9/11

Ironically, the attack on the Twin Towers occurred on the same calendar date as the Chilean coup in 1973, which, as outlined above, has often been seen as synonymous with the start of the neoliberal experiment. The second 9/11, while not signalling neoliberalism's downfall, has been synonymous with a period where the optimism of the 1990s has turned into pessimism. Even Fukuyama was forced to admit that his initial statement that history was reaching its end was perhaps premature, as we had now entered an era that Michael Cox was to describe as the 'post-post cold war era' (Cox 2004). Not only did the wars in Afghanistan and in Iraq result in more resentment of US power, they also gave the impression that the USA was embarking upon a more explicit form of imperialism. In this way, the era from 9/11 through to the beginnings of the global financial crisis represented a more interventionist approach from the world's major superpower that would have a destabilizing effect on the neoliberal order.

The neoconservative response to the events of 9/11 was partly driven by a desire to preserve the legacy of free market neoliberalism that had thrived in the preceding decades. George W. Bush's State of the Union address in 2002 referring to an 'axis of evil' of rogue states that appeared confrontational to the USA led the international community to establish a precedent whereby any state which seemed to contest the legitimacy of the international system would risk potential military intervention. The neoconservative ideology, and the 'Project for the New American Century' that was at the forefront during the Bush administration, gave the impression that for the neoliberal agenda to succeed it would, after all, require the backing of a strong American presence. Or to return to Gramsci, it would rely on coercion as opposed to consent. For when hegemony cannot be achieved through consent, dominant groups can revert to coercive means (Gramsci 1971: 12).[3]

The 'Project for the New American Century' was initially devised and set up as a think tank critical of the manner in which the Clinton administration had managed foreign affairs during the 1990s. Subscribed to by a number of traditional intellectuals that included politicians such as Donald Rumsfeld and Dick Cheney, policy advisers such as Elliott Adams and Fred Iklé and academics such as Donald Kagan and Eliot Cohen, and aided by journals such as *National Interest* and *Foreign Affairs*, it argued that greater military spending and intervention were required in order to ensure that the liberal peace that had been secured at the end of the Cold War obtained. Endorsed by Fukuyama, the group warned of the commercial and security danger to liberal democracy, owing to the emergence of dangerous and inhospitable governments in certain parts of the world.[4] When Bush was returned as president, his initial outlook seemed to indicate that he favoured more of an isolationist approach to international politics, but the events of 9/11 saw an interventionist U-turn and many from the 'Project for the New American Century' gained considerable influence in his administration. The Bush administration moved from a war against the Taliban and against al-Qaeda to one fought over alleged weapons of mass destruction. It also bought a new normative dimension whereby the USA had a moral obligation to defend the ethos of freedom and liberty. As a result, Bush's interventionism managed to unite the notion of strategic defence against external foes with a duty to lead the world towards universal liberty.

What emerged through this was a moulding of old-fashioned realist ideas with a new vision of liberal idealism. Traditional international relations scholars were finding it difficult to ascertain whether George W. Bush was a realist or an idealist (Mazaar 2003). Realists are noted for mistrust of international institutions and a commitment to state-centric solutions, which the bypassing of endorsement by the United Nations Security Council over the invasion of Iraq would tend to demonstrate. Yet the belief in American international leadership and in a crusade against illiberal rogue states is something that would appear at odds with the realist rationale, and one that is firmly an idealist commitment. The approach was possibly best summed up by the neoconservative columnist Charles Krauthammer. He suggested that what was happening after 9/11 was a form of 'democratic realism' that was both necessary and unique to the post-Cold War period. As the world had changed into a unipolar one – where one state wields significantly more power than any other in the system – then the USA had to use this position in a strategic and moral way (Krauthammer 2004). This included a rejection of institutionalism, as it provided a means for encouraging enemies, and a reaffirmation that the state power of the unipolar state – the USA – was the true source of intervention.

For Krauthammer, and indeed for all neocons, intervention and regime change were a means to democratize states that were ideologically threatening to the USA and to 'liberty', and to provide another stepping stone towards the universal liberal democratic end of history. Yet the move brought a whole new set of comments from all sides of the political spectrum that a new form of imperialism or American empire was being implemented.[5] The neoconservative response was to deny any imperialist gain and hold firm to the line that the USA was a world leader and constitutionally and ideologically opposed to the notion of imperialism. Yet criticisms that have followed point to the fact that the USA has tended to target energy-rich states so that a more US-friendly administration can provide easier access for US companies to secure beneficial oil contracts. While the charge of imperialism was levelled from one position, a further charge of US strategic overstretch has been levelled from another. The argument here is that an emerging multipolar world would weaken US power if it maintained its expansive approach. The rise of China and the reconstruction of other regional power bases would erode the position of the USA in world affairs. This position is one that emerged within conservative circles and is very much rooted in a belief in American isolationism and that the USA should retreat towards a policy of retrenchment.

The shift in outlook after 9/11 also saw a move to a belief that the world is heading towards a 'clash of civilizations' and away from the 'end of history' rhetoric that was popular before. This originates from Samuel Huntington's antithesis to the end of history, in which he argues that post-Cold War the world will be divided into cultural regions, often based on religious beliefs that are destined to conflict with each other (Huntington 1996). Suddenly, in the immediate aftermath of the attacks on September 11th, his book became hot property, with his analysis being referred to by the media, politicians and policy advisers. But following this new prediction of gloom, how have events after 9/11 affected the nature of neoliberal hegemony? As stated above, on the one hand the interventionism by the USA was conceived by many to be either a show of imperialism or, if we return to Gramsci, a demonstration of coercion. The problem with adopting this type of force is that if it fails to lead to a stable outcome, contestation can be more profound. The failure to stabilize the places where the USA intervened has obviously led to the sharp rise in resistance groups and militancy. The sense of a cultural clash has been heightened by the rise in religious forms of resistance that have emerged as a serious ideological challenge to the ascendancy of neoliberalism (see Chapter 5). Closer to home, Bush's policies and the pursuit of unipolarity increased the forms of discontent that were building up through the anti-capitalist movements, and these further widened the cracks that emerged over the legitimacy of neoliberalism.

The failure of Bush's interventionist crusade was becoming noticeable well before the end of his administration. The inability to bring the US presence in Iraq to a successful conclusion weighed heavily on the administration. The 'Project for the New American Century' disbanded in 2006 and was replaced by the less renowned and significantly less well-backed 'Foreign Policy Initiative'. By the end of the Bush administration, a new crisis had emerged that was to take centre stage in global affairs and severely test the very fabric of neoliberalism.

In July 2007, the global investment bank Bear Stearns disclosed that their hedge funds had made huge losses, and what is now known as the global financial crisis began to occur.

The consequences of the global financial credit crisis for the idea of neoliberalism are central to this book and are discussed at length elsewhere, but for us to judge the nature of neoliberal hegemony, it must be understood in the context from which it was coming. From a historical perspective we can see that the neoliberal experiment was something that was conceived in the immediate aftermath of the Second World War, unleashed in Anglo-Saxon countries in the 1980s, but didn't gain ascendancy until the end of the Cold War. After 9/11, neoliberalism was often associated, rightly or wrongly, with US intervention and a conviction that, when necessary, it can call upon coercion as well as consent to attempt to secure its growth (Harvey 2003). Yet the backlash that started with a questioning of the principles of free market economics was extended to the attack on the US-led military intervention in the Middle East. This was the background to how the world found itself prior to the start of the financial crisis. By the time the financial crisis occurred, the neoliberal project was already being contested on grounds of inequality, for being undemocratic, for subverting national identities and sovereignty, as a weapon of US-led imperialism, and for appearing to be the enemy of a specific religious belief. The global financial crisis was to lead to a deepening of these criticisms and to the charge that it was unsustainable as a form of economic governance. Yet, as I will show, the inability of these criticisms to construct a clear alternative to neoliberalism has allowed it to continue on its journey.

History and the Last Man

Fukuyama's end of history proclamation was followed up with his book *The End of History and the Last Man*, in which he pondered whether humanity might not once more plunge itself into another set of conflicts or whether it would be content with the spirit of liberalism (Fukuyama 1992: 287–314). If we are entering the phase of the 'Last Man' then the form of liberalism that has been prescribed has some way to go before this goal is achieved. The form of liberal democracy that was to gain supremacy was that of free market idealism, ideologic- ally conceived by economic market theorists who were to become key figures in their field. In practice, this form of 'neoliberalism' was not something that was compatible with the emancipating ideals of a De Tocqueville or a Mill, but was often more successful when practised alongside authoritarianism. Yet this is what had emerged as the dominant model of political economy in light of the Soviet collapse and found particular favour with states that did not have a developed democratic formation.

Looking at it from a Marxian perspective, neoliberalism was primarily a class project. If the mobilization of the working classes from the end of the nineteenth century led to a series of concessions that resulted in the Keynesian settlement post-1945, then the process of neoliberalism has represented a response from big business and from capital. Yet this could not be achieved without the construction of hegemony and common sense. The rediscovery of individualism and of the Protestant ethos of work, the commitment to the global market and to the practices of globalization, have all contributed to market-based forms of class consent. Culturally, national customs, religious belief and other forms of identity have managed to become assimilated into the wider market mentality.

However, despite the commercial success of neoliberalism, the social consequences have now put it firmly on the defensive. Inequality at a global level has risen consistently since the 1970s (Held and Kaya 2007), and those few states (such as France) which have bucked this trend have been ones that have been slow to discard their existing models of economic development (OECD 2011). The consequences of World Bank/IMF intervention have often led to an increase in social degeneration and have failed to lift states out of poverty. Within the developed world, the attempt at an '*embourgeoisement*' of society has led to a rapid growth of an underclass which governments have failed to reduce with market solutions. In some cases (such as those of Russia or Argentina in the late 1990s/early 2000s), the fallout from the neoliberal experimentation was such that it put a permanent dent in any idea that it could produce a utopian worldwide solution.

In *Thus Spoke Zarathustra*, Nietzsche's Last Man was one that was so weak willed that he became apathetic to his surroundings and was prepared to settle for the society around him (Nietzsche 2006). Fukuyama drew from Nietzsche, but saw the Last Man as one who could turn to liberal democracy and the free market as offering the best solution for humanity and would hail its universality as opposed to struggling against it (Fukuyama 1992: 313–22). However, the practical reality of neoliberalism is such that if it is not contested then Nietzsche's vision of the Last Man would be more apt than Fukuyama's, and it is not then surprising that resistance has emerged to challenge the nature of global capitalism. The nature, form and, more importantly, relevance of such resistance are discussed in the next chapter.

2 | RESISTANCE AND COUNTER-HEGEMONY

> The only people we hate more than the Romans are the fucking *Judean People's Front* (John Cleese as Reg, leader of the People's Front of Judea, *Life of Brian*, 1979)

If neoliberal economic globalization found itself the hegemonic political force in global political economy after the end of the Cold War, then the process of resistance was one that drew interest quickly from social scientists. The process and understanding of resistance have been added to many studies of globalization and have been the subject of many books and articles. The first observation to make regards the nature of globalization itself. As Barry Gills correctly puts it, 'the paradox of neoliberal economic globalisation is that it both weakens and simultaneously activates the social forces of resistance' (Gills 2000: 3). The logic of this is telling. For on one level neoliberalism has become an all-encompassing force that has given the impression that, to paraphrase Margaret Thatcher, there is no alternative. On another, the results of globalization have been that as the world has 'shrunk' through the enhancement of technology then so has the possibility of resistance. Indeed, the main acts of resistance that have occurred at a transnational level have all been facilitated through the aid of technology and the Internet. From the Zapatistas' uprising in Mexico to the recent 'Occupy' movement, and from the attack on the World Trade Center to anti-Islamic protests in western Europe, global forms of communication have been key to their emergence and existence.

If global forms of communication have allowed resistance to organize, they also led to it being fragmented and diverse. Globalization has been understood in a variety of ways, and discontent with it has been expressed in equally diverse ways. The interpretation of what 'globalization' is and how 'neoliberalism' is understood often defines the very nature and substance of resistance groups. This is explained very well by Manuel Castells, when he looks at how different social movements and identities have been constructed in ways that contest the hegemony of neoliberalism and seek to either shield themselves from the excesses of the global market, or to transform it (Castells 1997). In the second book of his trilogy on the Network Society, Castells notes that the post-Cold War world has been one where there has been a breakdown of the social relations that were evident during twentieth-century paternalism, to be replaced by a world where traditional identities are being eroded. For Castells, it has been the disenfranchisement that has emerged as a result of the loss of these identities, coupled with the influx of technology, which has resulted in the emergence of fragmenting forms of resistance. As he argues:

> Globalisation and informationalisation, enacted by networks of wealth, technology, and power, are transforming our world. They are enhancing our productive capability, cultural creativity, and communication potential. At the same time, they are disfranchising societies. As institutions of state and organisations of civil society are based on culture, history, and geography, the sudden accelera-tion of the historical tempo, and the abstraction of power in a web of computers, are disintegrating existing mechanisms of social control and political representation. (Ibid.: 68–9)

It is questionable whether the impact of globalization and techno-logy has had quite the social transformation that Castells suggests, but as we saw in the last chapter, the end of the Cold War altered the way in which socio-political and socio-economic relations were expressed. The clash of ideology that had previously dominated has left a vacuum that has been taken up by several different types of contestation. This can make it increasingly difficult to analyse both the form and the context of resistance as new forms of social move-ments have emerged that have often not been rooted in the same historical traditions as those in the past. For the so-called network society allows relationships and networks to be formed that do not necessarily have a shared spatial, ethnic, religious or national identity.

Several theories have been put forward on how we can approach the notion of resistance. I shall show that, while new forms of resistance have emerged through contrasting means, they can still nevertheless be categorized loosely into quite familiar traditions. Likewise, while there have been a number of unique ways in which resistance can be categorized, I believe that the Marxian form of resistance that was developed by Gramsci remains the most useful.

Conceptualizing resistance

As I indicated above, there has been much material published on how resistance to forms of neoliberalism can be conceptualized in the era of globalization, and there are many very well-researched pieces of work that have recently emerged on the nature of globalization and its contestation that I do not have the space to mention here.[1] One useful departure point for appreciating how resistance can be understood comes from the typological account provided by Christine Chin and James Mittelman. They argue that resistance can be analysed in three different ways which can also be seen in part as being compatible. These are through Gramsci's uses of counter-hegemony, through Polanyi's understanding of the counter-movement, and through James C. Scott's bottom-up understanding of hidden transcripts or infrapolitics (Chin and Mittelman 2000).

Counter-hegemony The process of counter-hegemony is pretty self-explanatory, in the context of the explanation of hegemony in Chapter 1. Counter-hegemonic movements are ideological projects that seek to challenge the common sense of hegemony through the dual actions of what Gramsci referred to as the 'war of movement' and the 'war of position' (Gramsci 1971: 229–35). The former refers to what Chin and Mittelman call a 'frontal assault against the state' and includes armed insurrections, mass protests, strikes, etc., while the latter refers to the more implicit form of protests (boycotts, the contestation of ideas, etc.) (Chin and Mittelman 2000: 32–4). A counter-hegemonic project would be one resting on a strong ideology that could receive strong support within civil society. As indicated in the first chapter, the role of organic intellectuals is important in forming the consciousness of a specific ideology, and this would have to be strongly evident if a counter-hegemonic project were to be successful.

There have been a number of accounts that have used the concept of counter-hegemony to understand resistance to neoliberal globalism (Rupert 2000; Gill 2000; Worth 2002; Worth and Abbott 2006) and have argued that it is a very useful method of understanding how the transformation of world order can occur. It should be said, however, that Gramsci's own use of the term was largely (and debatably) for a specific purpose. The term 'counter-hegemony' is not really employed – at least as a distinct term – by Gramsci in the notebooks, and his understanding of the process of hegemony was central to his idea of building a socialist society. There have been arguments made by neo-Gramscians in the past that a post-hegemonic world, based upon a form of democratic global governance, can be the result of counter-hegemonic engagement (Cox 1996), but this differed from Gramsci's own understanding of hegemony. To an extent Gramsci was building upon previous notions of hegemony that were being formed by leading Marxists at the time. For example, Lenin understood hegemony as a necessary tool for order within the confines of the socialist state (Joseph 2002: 48–50), while Rosa Luxemburg moved the question on to how hegemony consciousness and contestation within the socialist movement are more effective through workers' cooperatives (Laclau and Mouffe 1985: 8–14). Gramsci's main objective was to build an *alternative* hegemony to that which was practised in capitalist society.

While it would be doctrinaire to go too far in highlighting the differences between 'counter-hegemony' and the idea of an 'alternative hegemony', it does have some relevance to our discussions on understanding resistance today. Spread consistently through Gramsci's notebooks are many micro-studies of practices within Italian society that contribute to Italian hegemony and to the fashioning of common sense.[2] He wanted to demonstrate the depths that an alternative socialist project would have to go to before it could challenge the existing hegemonic relationships. He argued that many of the Marxist contributions to building consent within socialist society negated these complexities. Nikolai Bukharin's highly influential *Popular Manual* comes in for particular criticisms. In it he suggests that the subaltern masses would spontaneously reject the philosophy/ideology of the ruling classes – once they gained a sense of class consciousness. Gramsci, however, argues that such a 'clean break' from the philosophies of the ruling classes is impossible because the popular masses are actually organically tied to the philosophy and ideologies of the ruling classes – past and present (Gramsci 1971: 184–90). Likewise, while applauding Rosa Luxemburg's vision in identifying economic action such as mass strikes as a form of economic resistance, he also added that this only went as far as understanding the nature of the war of movement; the war of position was far more complex and could not be reduced to economism (Gramsci 2007: 161–2).

What is very obvious in Gramsci's criticisms of such prominent Marxists is that his understanding of transformation was radically different from that of the majority working within the socialist movement at the time in the sense that, in his understanding, an alternative hegemonic movement would have to develop a form of common sense distinctive enough to challenge all facets of everyday life. In the contemporary environment, therefore, we would be looking at an alternative or counter-hegemony project that would have not just a firm ideological direction, but would need to be combined with a series of what Gramsci termed 'national-popular' incentives. These would be formulated through a strong network and a balance of traditional and organic intellectuals. Counter-hegemony is, in my opinion, the most useful departure point for us to understand and locate the strength of contestation to dominant forms of hegemony, and it also gives us some idea of the limits and potential of a specific form of resistance.

Counter-movement The idea of a 'counter-movement' stems from Karl Polanyi's seminal study on nineteenth-century English society and from the birth of the self-regulated market economy. In the book *The Great Transformation*, he argued that the problems of the first half of the twentieth century can be traced back to the refusal of states to interfere with the overall fabric of market rule. In complete contrast to the Hayekian argument outlined in Chapter 1, Polanyi argued that it was the dependency on the market system that ultimately led to its collapse. For as the market was left to self-regulate, then it was constantly being met by calls for re-regulation as society sought to protect itself from the excesses of the market system. The period of nineteenth-century market development was therefore governed by a 'double movement', whereby the market system was met by a series of 'counter-movements', which ultimately brought it down (Polanyi 2001 [1944]: 136). In the nineteenth century, these 'counter-movements' included Chartism in industrial Britain and the labour movement and welfare reforms across the whole of Europe. It was the starkest of all counter-movements, however, that of fascism, which was to emerge as the movement that signalled the end of market society.

The similarities between the crisis of nineteenth-century liberalism and contemporary neoliberalism are quite obvious at first sight, and Polanyi's critique of the former undoubtedly gives us plenty to ponder on today (Hann and Hart 2009). Indeed, the inability of states and leaders to see beyond the overriding principles of market rule makes for very telling similarities with those who swore by the infallibility of the gold standard. Yet using the 'counter-movement' as a way of understanding contemporary forms of market contestation is not without its problems. First, a coherent counter-movement would require an organizational structure and a unified set of objectives. These were found in groups such as Chartism in the nineteenth century and, to a degree, the wider fascist movement in the twentieth century. While certain NGOs can be interpreted as meeting these criteria, many movements in the contemporary technological age have an appearance of 'submerged networks' in that they are loosely connected through shared ideals and cannot bear any comparisons with similar movements in Polanyi's era (Chin and Mittelman 2000; Birchfield and Freyberg-Inan 2004).

One could actually go farther than outlining the problems contemporary movements might have in replicating movements from a bygone age and suggest that Polanyi's own use of the 'counter-movement' is actually overplayed. The term is used only in *The Great Transformation* and it is questionable just how much emphasis he put on the term. For instance, the examples given as forms of counter-movements in the book, such as the Chartists and the growth of workers' unions, were largely shown as specific historical instances responding to a free market system that Polanyi felt was unsustainable. Most of these led to democratic or social reforms which were brought about owing to the unstable nature of the self-regulated market system. Polanyi's argument was that such reforms that were subsequently endorsed by the British parliament could not function alongside a market system as they were contradictory in their very nature and outlook. His final premise was that such a system had now been defeated and was one that would be considered as the nineteenth-century understanding of civilization (Polanyi 2001 [1944]: 257–68). I feel therefore that it is questionable to argue that the counter-movement acts as a theoretical mechanism in understanding market resistance as it was applied in *The Great Transformation* as historical instances. The fact that the forms of neoliberal market governance developed in the contemporary era have managed to adapt to factors such as universal suffrage, union rights, the welfare state,[3] etc., means that any attempt to utilize a theory of the counter-movement would have to do a considerable amount of work historicizing and specifying the concept (Worth 2012).

Despite this, the general principles behind the idea of the counter-movement remain as prevalent as before. Polanyi's critique of free market economies and the conviction that its expression will inevitably lead to forms of contestation and resistance remain as relevant today as they did in the nineteenth century. At the same time, accounts have also shown ways in which the Gramscian-inspired form of counter-hegemony can be used alongside the concept of the counter-movement. This has been done in order to understand resistance at a level that incorporates the more classical Marxist approach of Gramsci with the more sociological approach of market critique in order to produce a wider understanding of how and why resistance occurs within contemporary capitalist societies (Burawoy 2003).

Critical movements The third form of conceptualization that Chin and Mittelman develop explores the work of James Scott, which can be placed alongside forms of resistance understood 'from below' that have been developed from a diverse body of thought that has work influenced by Foucault, libertarian Marxism and postmodernism. While these positions might conflict theoretically, they all focus upon resistance from below that does not necessarily have a unified ideological position regarding transformation. They also concentrate on the different levels that occur within patterns of resistance. They can range from those within a central power at the top of a social structure to those at the lower level, which can be considered as being within the politics of everyday life.

Scott's work on the subaltern classes suggests that those that are dominated tend to resist rather than contest rule by the dominators. At first examination this appears to contrast with Gramsci's concept, as societies are not shaped by practices that bind them to a passive relationship between dominant and subaltern classes, but instead are marked by constant struggle. On closer inspection, there are areas that Scott observes can be included in a wider Gramscian analysis. For, as works by Gramscians in cultural studies have demonstrated, hegemony is a process that is constantly being contested (Hall and Jefferson 1993). Indeed, as Stuart Hall's well-known studies on the building of Thatcherism in Britain demonstrate, hegemonic consent is an open-ended process whereby cultures and subcultures are constantly contesting its processes. The war of position is one whereby hegemonic consent is achieved only through the constant defence and renewal of a specific strategic project (Hall 1988; Rupert 2000: 13–14).

In terms of his overall understanding of resistance, however, Scott has more in common with Foucault. Foucault's perception of power in social relations provides an altogether different meaning of resistance. For Foucault, resistance occurs everywhere a power relation exists. Yet as power is dispensed and directed within separate discourses there are no unified causes or universal expressions of such resistance but rather 'a plurality of resistances, each of them a special case' (Foucault 1998 [1979]: 96). As a result, Foucauldians can account for any form and type of resistance at every level, but they place a different emphasis on their form and significance. Yet it is questionable how much significance the outcomes of such resistance might achieve. From one position, you could say that, as forms of resistance can challenge power relations at any level of society, then they have the ability to challenge the prevailing conditions in which such relationships are constructed. From another, however, you could argue that as power relations are dispersed across all layers of society, can any form of resistance make any significant difference? Again, here we refer to the overriding principles of neoliberalism in questioning whether such forms of resistance can contest these larger processes. Some Foucauldian or postmodernist accounts might reject such a concept altogether, at least beyond the realms of a constructed narrative. Yet Foucault applied a great deal of effort to looking at the manner in which power or 'biopower' has been utilized so that neoliberal principles can be projected as an 'art of governance' by states and significant actors (Foucault 2008: 130–2). It is perhaps best to regard the resistance to these projections as ones which can articulate critical forms that can lead to different forms and strategies of contestation.

Such critical movements can be understood as those which appear at the bottom-up level of analysis and stimulate activities that articulate forms of dissent. These include forms of protest, but also actions which take place at the level of everyday life that might occur in the workplace or the domestic social sphere. Examples of protest movements here include the growth of the culture and subculture that have been inherent within the anti-capitalist movements. Groups that have recently stressed the need to 'reclaim space' from corporate ownership in urban areas draw many of their ideas from the Situationist International movement that originated in the aftermath of the Paris student protests of 1968. Associated with the work of Guy Debord, the Situationist International (SI) coupled the utopian anti-art tradition that had its roots in the Dadaist movement fifty years previously with the practice of systemic resistance. SI principles such as *détournement* (the tactic of subverting images) and psychogeography (using space to artistically express resistance) have been actively pursued by contemporary forms of protest, through acts such as graffiti and the use of images (Debord 2002; Worth and Abbott 2006). From the birth of what was called the anti-globalization movement at Seattle, through to the anti-war demonstrations against Bush's interventionist foreign policy, and the recent 'Occupy' movements resulting from the financial crisis, artistic forms of expressing protest coupled with the commitment to occupy and reclaim urban space have been evident.

Critical movements can also embrace civil struggles that occur through empowerment groups or within women's groups. The work of Cynthia Enloe, for example, has reminded us that power relations are also gendered and that behind every struggle at the subaltern level there is also a gendered one that is evident from the margins of the social sphere of interaction to the central powers of global politics (Enloe 1996). Indeed, while the gendered struggles might be formulated within the arrangement of paternalism that saturates society as a whole, the increase in gendered wage inequality and the growing use of the pink-collared worker in production demonstrates the gendered nature of the larger neoliberal project. Critical movements thus facilitate any form of contestation at every level of society and pursue both different strategies and different outcomes. They are considered jointly in analysis only by virtue of the fact that they all contest the wider social relationship that they are working within.

Can these more implicit critical movements actually provide us with an alternative or further layer of analysis in terms of understanding contemporary resistance? I feel they can, but only placed within, rather than opposed to, a wider Marxian analysis of hegemony/counter-hegemony. Those who might go down the post-structural road or more extensively down the road of discourse theory might conclude that these critical movements show that there is no one central form of hegemony and that there can be no overall substantive connection between resistance at these different layers of society (Walker 1994). However, as others have shown, it is only by considering them within a wider class-based analysis that these movements become relevant. Drawing on the same form of enquiry as Marxist historians such as E. P. Thompson, André Drainville shows how the different class struggles occur through different spheres of activity within urban production. In doing so, he shows how in what he calls 'world cities', which form the hub of capitalist hegemonic consent, resistance has been forged through everyday struggles and upon different terrains (Drainville 2004). Through his studies of London and New York in the nineteenth century and of Quebec City at the turn of the twenty-first century he shows the different stages of the development of the global city. He also shows how attempts to resist the character of their growth developed from the strikes in London of the 1890s to the situationist-inspired tactics of anti-capitalist protesters in the contemporary era, and how such struggles have led the dominant classes to respond in restoring the fabric of social relations, which are presented as being increasingly global in scope (ibid.: 105–39).

In essence, what Drainville does with resistance and with the contestation of hegemony, Hall did with the construction of hegemony. Both use Marx and Gramsci as a departure point and both account for the everyday struggle to maintain the fight for hegemony. Hall's studies of Thatcherite Britain and of British subcultures are applied through what he terms 'Marxism without guarantees'. Here, he argues that while class structures are shaped by economic action in the 'first instance', the open forms of civil and cultural struggle provide the battleground for their respective legitimization (Hall 1996: 42–5). At times of instability, the weaknesses of this hegemonic legitimacy are exploited through the forms of the war of position and the war of movement that Drainville demonstrates through his studies of contemporary resistance. The populist forms of consent that were achieved in Thatcher's Britain, which Hall explores, are understood in the same open context as Drainville explores when looking at the contemporary neoliberal protest. It is through these wider Gramscian studies that we can make sense of the complexities that exist when looking at resistance, and they allow us to unite the various forms of conceptualizations that Chin and Mittelman outline and which I have explored here.

Types of resistance

If we can argue that resistance can be understood through contesting the hegemony of a specific order, then how does this allow us to locate the forms of resistance that are evident today? A broader Gramscian framework might allow us to look at some of the levels of contestation that others might ignore, but that does not get us closer to assessing what general types of resistance exist. Indeed, one could also ask, as resistance is evident at so many levels of society, can we comfortably suggest that different ideological forms of resistance similarly and categorically exist?

The answer to that question is yes, but that does not necessarily mean that each has a strong basis for a hegemonic challenge. As outlined above, for a counter-hegemonic challenge to emerge as a substantive threat to the existing order it needs to have a clear ideological alternative and sustain a balance between the wars of movement and position. Indeed, rather than creating division, critical movements should provide an important mechanism for this to be achieved. There have been a number of ideological criticisms of neoliberalism and it remains highly problematic to broadly categorize them into distinct forms when deep divisions exist within them. However, as I will show in terms of outcomes, there are generally three types of resistance: progressive internationalism, national-populism and religious fundamentalism. The three can be distinguished by the manner in which they view global capitalism and the way in which they would like to see it transformed.

Progressive internationalism Progressive internationalism includes all those forms of resistance that seek to transform contemporary capitalism through social intervention. To borrow from Polanyi, it is a commitment to embedding the economy within social relations rather than vice versa. It is also a belief that global governance should radically alter its neoliberal appearance. Included here would be groups and individuals involved in the anti-capitalist movements, NGOs and civil societal groups from both the developed and the developing worlds, reformists, international socialists and anarchists. This would indeed categorize nearly all those that are commonly associated with those from the left that are critical of unfettered capitalism.

Yet in order to mount a hegemonic challenge a left-wing strategy would need to present a substantive coalition that establishes a clear agenda on how the current order should be contested and what a new post-neoliberal order would look like. There are obviously huge ideological discrepancies in how an alternative might be constructed and what it might look like. Perhaps two of the best illustrations of this can be seen in the respective accounts by Alex Callinicos on one side and David Held/Anthony McGrew on the other. Callinicos, a long-time active member of the UK Socialist Workers Party, outlines six different types of anti-capitalist agendas, and five of the six would fit into the category of progressive internationalism. These are bourgeois anti-capitalism, localist anti-capitalism, globalist anti-capitalism, reformist anti-capitalism, autonomist anti-capitalism and socialist anti-capitalism (Callinicos 2003: 70–86). The only other category that he mentions is reactionary anti-capitalism, which appears at odds with the other varieties of resistance (ibid.: 68–70). This does highlight ideological divisions, although some strands of contestation, such as bourgeois anti-capitalism (ibid.: 71–3), facilitate a role that could perhaps better be described as one that promotes corporate responsibility, and a further four more (globalist anti-capitalism, reformist anti-capitalism, autonomist anti-capitalism and socialist anti-capitalism) are not necessarily divided on levels of strategy rather than on ideology.

David Held and Anthony McGrew have both been associated with the cosmopolitan movement and with the idea of global democratization. Their understanding of the diversity of resistance to global capitalism is expressed through a matrix of different intellectual positions. For them, progressive critiques of neoliberalism can be understood as having cosmopolitans at one end of the spectrum and communitarians at the other. They also range from the top to the bottom, with globalists at the top and sceptics at the bottom (Held and McGrew 2007: 164). They suggest that radicals that make up the majority of positions that Callinicos outlined remain largely in the centre, while traditional statist social democrats may spawn reactionary or nationalist movements. As a result, cosmopolitan democracy remains the most viable course of action as it not only transforms the appearance of global capitalism, but also uses the social and cultural dimensions of globalization to facilitate a transformation of the traditional 'outdated' nation-state system of governance (ibid.: 187, 206–20).

What seems to be emerging from these debates is the general distinction between those who largely understand that a hegemonic challenge is more likely to come from gradual transformation and those who believe in a more radical form of revolutionary change. As Callinicos himself acknowledges, this represents an age-old dilemma between those who believe in gradual reform of a specific system and those who argue that the system itself needs to be replaced. Yet, historically, the ideological fabrics of the different radical groups have also served to blight the left. The splits between different forms of groups based upon state socialism, syndicalism, anarchism and Marxism have long weakened any unified attempt to challenge an existing hegemonic project. Any strong form of counter-hegemony would not only have to resolve the ideological disparities that exist between those who favour a progressive global transformation, but would also have to coordinate firm suggestions on how this might be implemented. For while Callinicos himself might suggest ways in which this might be achieved, many have failed to do so, as I will explain later (Callinicos 2003: 132–9).

National populism The antithesis of the progressive global challenge to neoliberalism is one which argues that its actions produce a considerable threat to national forms of culture and life. It is one that is based upon the restoration of traditional national communities as a means of resisting change from above. For a strong hegemonic project based upon the principles of national populism to challenge an existing order, it needs to utilize a set of beliefs and interpretations that are based largely upon myth and on the politics of fear and loathing (Rupert 2000).

National-populist resistance does not necessarily have a combined set of strategies at the level of global governance, as the overall objective at that level is to diffuse and discourage any integration. Instead, what is required is a set of aggressive agendas based upon the nature of the bounded community. This is largely based on forms of nationalism but can also be formed around larger ethnicities or certain forms of exceptionalism. Unity between each group is not required at an international level; indeed, owing to the confrontational nature of the competing sets of communities, one of the defining virtues of this form of counter-hegemony is that it relies upon the distrust and sometimes revulsion of other bounded communities for its own clarity. Yet certain families of groups that share the same aim can be united in certain ways. For example, far-right movements in Europe have long created links and networks, often based on ethnicity. Fascism and its variants were unified through its appropriation of white Anglo-Saxon supremacy, while Serbian ethnicity has been keen to proclaim a 'brotherhood' between states that claim Serbian heritage. In addition, in order to secure the widespread growth of nationalism and global disunity, then the success of such a project relies upon this process occurring across a wide range of areas.

The problems with locating this type of resistance in the global political economy are numerous. For, as we shall see in Chapter 4, groups that have been associated with the 'far right' are not necessarily at odds with neoliberal economics. Despite the fact that there are many examples in the areas of International Political Economy and the politics of resistance that highlight the role reactionary groups play in neoliberal contestation (Rupert 2000; Worth 2002; Steger 2005), this has gone unrecognized in the field of comparative politics. Here, the growth of far-right parties is largely explained as being a result of immigration and multiculturalism, alongside a social belief in strong law and order and excessive welfarism. The last of these in particular would suggest support for wider market policies, and indeed it was a common misconception in the early 1990s within comparative politics that the far right were broadly supporting a neoliberal agenda (Betz 1994). Yet, as Cas Mudde argues, while the position of the economy appears to be of secondary importance, the opposition to what is understood as 'globalization' remains central to the appeal of this approach (Mudde 2007: 184–8). It is indeed this fear of what globalism will bring which forms the initial basis for a national-populist alternative, rather than a firm economic strategy. The economic positions of retraction and protection often follow once the social and civil battle lines are drawn.

Religious fundamentalism The religious fundamentalist challenge to neoliberalism might draw on some of the myths that inform the beliefs behind populist nationalism, but it also draws on a distinctly globalist perspective. For a counter-hegemonic response to successfully challenge the legitimacy of neoliberalism, it would need to establish a firm counter-ideology based on specific interpretations of religious belief. This at once leaves us with a set of questions on the sustainability of a religious-based challenge.

First, while Islamic fundamentalism is often regarded as the major contributor to religious ideological resistance to contemporary capitalism, there are other forms that are not associated with resistance. Hinduism and more prominently Christianity have both been recently associated with fundamentalist revival. As Castells shows in his study of the Aum Shinrikyo movement that gained notoriety through a gas attack on the Tokyo subway in 1995, specific readings of religious belief fused with the growth of a cult movement can create resistance through fear and terror, despite having a very small base of support (Castells 1997: 102–4). Therefore, religious-based forms of resistance are unlikely to be singular in character unless one specific religion gains influence over the others, as Christianity did with the aid of European colonialism from the fifteenth century onwards.

Secondly, religion, as Gramsci is quick to remind us, is a form of agency that can be used both to embed and complement an existing hegemonic system, and something that can be used as a form of resistance against it (Gramsci 1995: 1–138). Islamic fundamentalism is often presented in the manner exemplified by Huntington or Benjamin Barber (the author of *Jihad vs McWorld*), which is to suggest a clash of specific cultures brought about by the decline of the state system and the rise of globalism. Yet many have commented that political Islam has been projected as a form of counter-hegemony only by those who fear the unknown (Evans 2011). The reality is that Islam, like Christianity, is largely embedded in existing passive relationships.

Finally, Gramsci himself understood religion as a key component that could be used as a form of mobilization towards a socialist hegemonic project. Understanding religion's potential role within socialism was at odds with the large majority of Marxist scholars at the time, and certainly with the hard-line approach that was set in the Soviet Union. Yet religious groups have facilitated a key role in socially progressive movements previously, as seen in their contribution to the anti-imperialist movements and in liberation theology. Religion can also offer a useful partnership in the promotion of free market ideology, seen in the recent growth of the 'prosperity gospel' (Murray 2012). Therefore, any religious-based project that offers a counter-hegemonic alternative needs to centralize its religious message in its overall agenda and show that its main critique is one based on the interpretation of religious scriptures and communicated through intellectuals.

Owing to the regional spread of specific religions throughout the world, the obstacles to creating a new world order based on one such reading of one such religion are obvious. However, the success of a religious fundamentalist project would largely be measured by how far it can successfully halt the trend of neoliberal globalization. If successful, this, in turn, could lead to its widespread fragmentation, which would have serious repercussions for the overall character of the global system.

Fragmentation

While these three positions can be distinguished in terms of their overall scope and objectives, there are obvious overlaps between certain elements in each of them. As a result respective political positions and movements have emerged that often fit comfortably into more than one of the categories mentioned above. In this way it is possible that the driving ideological force of one particular approach becomes diluted. At the same time, divisions within the broad ideological positions can pose additional problems when mounting a counter-hegemonic challenge to the dominant hegemonic position. These divisions have led to claims that there remains a lack of firm, viable proposals on which any alternative can be based. These can all add to an argument that dominant classes look for these weaknesses and respond by seeking a process of cooperation that Gramsci referred to as *trasformismo* (Gramsci 1971: 58).

As has been mentioned numerous times before, splits between left-wing organizations are legendary. Since the bitter and often violent arguments that have followed the movements that accompanied the birth of socialism, anarchism, communism and social democracy, the left has been notorious in creating divisions and splits. These have occurred not just through ideological and strategic political differences in respective movements and organizations, but often through a clash of individual selfish interests. These deep divisions do not confine themselves just to the left, however. Splits have been equally prone to occur within nationalist, populist and religious forms of contestation. Partly this trend has much to do with the nature of opposition itself. As many classical studies in political party formation have argued, traditional 'catch-all' parties, as opposed to organizations that are tied to specific ideologies, have generally been more successful (Lipset and Rokkan 1967). Indeed, the neoliberal project was largely propelled by political parties that appeared to be either 'catch-all' or traditionally the largest and most well developed in their respective countries. Previously, it was often the same influential parties which successfully managed the Keynesian order that preceded neoliberalism. This would suggest that a counter-hegemony project would benefit if the war of position could occur within the realms of dominant political parties. Yet this itself presents a dilemma, and the majority of such organizations have positioned themselves as entities that guard against such radicalism.

An increase in right–left rhetoric has also emerged in recent years that has led to further confusion when categorizing distinct forms of resistance. In particular, national-populist ontology often seeks to use certain criticisms that are generally associated with the left in order to assume a position that can be regarded as a form of *retorsion* (Taguieff 1994) – that is, to use or borrow an argument that has been appropriated by one body of thought, but then turn it against its intended origin for one's own purpose. For example, many reactionary arguments have used the departure points put forward by progressive or left-wing positions in order to use them for their own purposes. Both the Front National (FN) in France and the British National Party (BNP) in the UK have highlighted the negative effects that free market globalization is inflicting on contemporary society. Both also highlight the problems with inequality and with the wider polarization of society. For them, however, the return to a national bounded community and the reversal of global integration seem obvious solutions to accompany these criticisms, and their populist and simplistic message can strike emotional chords with the public.

The right–left blurring has been aided by groups and figureheads themselves, who have to some degree forged unholy alliances. This was certainly seen in the NAFTA and WTO positions in the USA, when Ralph Nader and Pat Buchanan made several joint ventures in their opposition to the institutions. Ralph Nader has long been a champion of the American left and had stood on the Green Party ticket for the 1996 presidential elections, while Pat Buchanan, a renowned arch-conservative, stood as the candidate for Ross Perot's Reform Party in the 2000 presidential elections. Yet, owing to their criticism of free trade and of global corporate power, the two became closer in their political campaigning, with both arguing that the mainstream candidates did not allow for wider ideological debates. As a result, both urged a degree of support for the other in order for wider issues such as globalization to be debated (Anti-Fascist Forum 2001). This unholy coalition between the pair continued with the Reform Party urging their voters to support Nader in 2004, in the absence of their own candidate. The left–right unholy alliance is not a new phenomenon within political campaigning. In the referendum for continued European Community membership in the UK in the 1970s, the left, spearheaded by Tony Benn, was partnered in urging a 'no' vote by Enoch Powell, the darling of the conservative right. Yet this was a single-issue campaign, and, more importantly, Benn took great care to distance himself from the reactionary right by refusing to share a platform with them. In contrast, the Nader–Buchanan alliance became entrenched within American politics through the establishment of an 'anti-free-trade' agenda.

These developments weaken potential alternative strategies as they confuse the boundaries that exist between competing ideologies and allow for them to be exploited. While broader coalitions might seem attractive, they are ultimately unsustainable and, owing to their unpopularity among their own supporters, often lead to further splits and fragmentation. This allows for an easier process of *trasformismo*. Gramsci used the term when considering the battle for hegemony in the process of Italian unification. Once a dominant group takes hegemonic control in a social relationship it can maintain and strengthen its position by absorbing some of the concerns expressed by competing groups without compromising its own position. Fragmentations and unholy alliances allow the dominant groups that maintain the principles of the present order to respond to certain areas of concern. During the boom era of economic growth, this became a reasonably straightforward process, as social concerns and concerns about a lack of identity were dealt with by commitments such as social inclusion through private–public partnership (see the previous chapter) and by 'progressive nationalism' and 'patriotism'. As we will also see in Chapter 4, concerns such as immigration have often been addressed as a way of deflecting the wider problems associated with neoliberalism. During the current era of crisis, these co-option tactics have become more difficult. Instead, dominant groups have often adopted a defensive position by exploiting the weak alternatives that have been put forward in response. This has become a recent feature of states and key actors in the global economy as they have responded to calls for a radical overhaul of their management by calling them unviable and unrealistic.

Conclusion

The nature of neoliberalism is such that it has led to a backlash of resistance that has appeared in contrasting forms, with contrasting objectives. Unlike in previous eras, however, the advent of mass communication has led to an irony in terms of its organizational capability. Greater forms of resistance have been aired and imagined in realms such as cyberspace, which has broken down the barriers of traditional mass representations of media production. At the same time, while such outlets have stimulated forms of resistance, they have also led to the expression of such resistance being more fragmented. While in previous eras discontent with prevailing orders was organized through collective action and within specific organizations, the network society (to borrow from Castells) has provided an arena where individual and less formal consent can be built. This has been seen in the different varieties of groups and individuals that have participated in post-Seattle 'anti-globalization' protests and the variety of positions that criticisms of neoliberalism have taken. At the same time, such discontent has often been marked by a fragmentation that has weakened the overall potential for change.

In this chapter I have looked at the various ways in which resistance in political and civil society has been understood in relation to neoliberal globalization. While fragmented and at times individualistic, resistance is best understood using Gramsci's dual understandings of the war of movement and the war of position. The different practices and cultures that occur during the process of resistance, and which might appear at the level of everyday life, all provide potential impetus for the war of position. It is through these processes that neoliberalism can come under attack, in particular through ideas and ideology that seek to contest and tear apart the very fabric of the common sense that neoliberalism has produced.

The three general forms of resistance to emerge as potential counter-hegemony contenders – progressive internationalism, national populism and religious fundamentalist – have been drawn from a variety of contrasting positions that, owing to their scope, are prone to clash with one another. For us to assess whether one of these positions can develop as a serious contender to the contemporary neoliberal order, we need to look at all three in greater depth. It is through observing the nature and the expression of the three positions that we can draw some conclusions about whether they appear to be significant challengers. Alternatively, their significance may give us some indication as to whether neoliberalism can sustain itself in its present form in the near future.

3 | ANOTHER WORLD IS POSSIBLE?

Replace capitalism with something nice (Popular slogan used in protest marches, first heard in the May Day protests in London, 2000)

The backlash against neoliberalism from 'below' is often understood as one that began in the Mexican jungle before spreading to the streets of Seattle, London, Quebec City and Genoa within the following decade. The uprising in Mexico was instigated by the signing of the North American Free Trade Agreement (NAFTA), while the initial forms of street protests were strategically positioned around specific international economic institutional meetings and summits. To a degree the responses have come as a result of attempts to institutionally embed the neoliberal rationale. Every move to further the process of converging norms around general free market principles has been met with resistance.

Yet, as we shall see, while the protests against these processes have been united in the manner of their critiques of contemporary capitalism, they are less united in terms of what an alternative world might look like and what form it might take. Here phrases such as 'postmodern Prince', postmodern socialisms, radical global civil society from below, cosmopolitanism and global democratization have appeared alongside traditional understandings of revolutionary socialism and radical libertarianism. Yet, as Manfred Steger has suggested, there are very definite strands that unite what we might term 'left' forms of protest. For at the centre of such a critique lies a concern with inequality and with the international division of wealth. It is this commitment to international egalitarianism which unifies the concerns over the nature of the global economy (Steger 2005: 93–5). Ontologically, they are united by the belief that free markets and unregulated capitalism widen the equality gap and increase the strength of corporate power. Their departure point is that it is the structural workings of global politics which are essentially creating greater inequality, and it is these which need to be either reformed or revolutionized in order to make a more just world.

Despite this, groups remain that fit into and associate themselves with the internationalist position, but appear more inward looking on closer inspection. For example, out of the great variety of social movements included within gatherings such as the World and European Social Forums, there are many organizations whose ultimate aim is self-determination. Several independence groups, such as Basque, Kurdish and Palestinian organizations, for example, have joined in the wider campaigns for 'another world', but their main focus remains one of self-determination. The campaigns for national self-determination may be situated within the context of what can be interpreted as a form of an anti-imperialist struggle or as a struggle against state oppression; they can also be understood within a more inward-looking nationalistic one. Such nationalist movements would stress the progressive nature of their respective campaigns and would distance themselves from the chauvinism of reactionary forms of nationalism that are distinctly at odds with global solutions. Yet they still stress traditional forms of self-determination that might – perhaps inadvertently – lead to cases of disintegration in global society of the type that would be welcomed by the more 'reactionary' forms of nationalism. For example, the rise of the left in South America has been instigated as a response to the growing Americanization of the region. Responses by leaders such as Hugo Chávez have attracted observations that a distinct difference exists between the cosmopolitan left and the 'left' that seems to borrow more from a populist nationalism associated with Bolívar or Perón than from those contrasting internationalists (Castaneda and Morales 2008; Steger 2005: 106–9). It is these moves which might lead to different consequences at the wider international level. Any move towards protectionism could precipitate a wider round of similar measures at the national or the regional level that would negate any wider commitments to global change. Thus, when looking at positions which associate themselves with the label 'progressive internationalism', certain campaigns and agendas have on closer inspection the potential to slip back towards a national-protectionist standpoint.

The Zapatistas

While the Zapatistas have been associated with the initial inspiration for the later anti-capitalist protest movement (Klein 2002), the movement itself was triggered by a clause in the NAFTA agreement that significantly put at risk indigenous rights to land. For the free trade agreement meant that Article 27 of the Mexican constitution, which had been historically forged in the aftermath of the 1910 revolution, had to be repealed. This ended the communal rights to indigenous agricultural ownership and opened it up to market competition. In addition, it was feared that the NAFTA agreement would halt the process of repatriation of native Indian land that had dated back to the famous campaigns of Emilio Zapata.

The insurrection that occurred on the morning of 1 January 1994 (the day that NAFTA came into effect) brought over three thousand men and women out to declare war on the Mexican state and to occupy specific municipal buildings within the Chiapas region in the south of the country. What followed was a violent clash with army reinforcements and the police that resulted in the group retreating to the jungle, proclaiming themselves to be guerrillas of the Ejército Zapatista de Liberación Nacional (EZLN). Subsequently, the Zapatistas have presented themselves as libertarian socialists whose struggles represent a dichotomy between the global and the local in the quest to challenge the ideology of neoliberalism. Headed by the self-proclaimed Subcomandante Marcos, a figure whose identity is concealed through the donning of a mask or balaclava, the group spent the next decade in and out of dialogue with respective Mexican governments, attempting to negotiate a solution to the land question. With no such solution forthcoming the Zapatistas have taken to declaring their own governing procedure in the Chiapas region, while the state has greatly increased the military presence in the area in order to stop the movement spreading its influence.

What the Zapatistas became noted for was that they a) appeared to bridge the local and global divide in the manner in which they understood politics; b) formed a type of resistance that represented a distinct break from guerrilla-based Marxist-Leninist campaigns of the past; and c) established a specific culture of protest that had not been witnessed before. In terms of the first, many of the key campaigns of the EZLN are pitched at, and rely upon, the international community. While some have argued that the Zapatistas might represent a type of postmodern movement that is becoming commonplace within global politics, but is ultimately concerned with its own specific objectives (Watson 2002), many have pointed to Marcos's rhetoric to insist that the group has a distinct international agenda. For example, the group's own political statements stress the commitment to resistance to the neoliberal doctrine at all levels of society, irrespective of borders and territorial boundaries (Zapatistas 1998: 11–13). Part of the appeal of the Zapatistas is that their resistance is universal in the sense that resistance to neoliberalism can occur at all levels depending on circumstances.

Ultimately, if the Zapatistas did stimulate a sense that resistance to neoliberalism could be utilized in a manner that encouraged both international solidarity and individual action tailored to specific campaigns, then how are these understood? Much has been written on the manner in which the Zapatistas have interpreted the idea of power. In different ways both John Holloway and Hardt and Negri have stressed the different nature of resistance campaigns in light of the activities of the EZLN and have shown us that the takeover (by any means) of the state no longer appears to be the final strategic political objective. By establishing forms of self-autonomy that reject the forming of social relations around capital, resistance can be empowered from below (Holloway 2002). To a degree the Zapatistas can be understood as a new form of resistance against the totality of the new ruling configuration of global politics, whereby institutional power and its civilly constituted parts have replaced previous understandings of the nation-state system (Hardt and Negri 2000). If, therefore, we are to believe that politics has undergone this shift in character in the last few decades, then previous revolutionary movements that were designed to take over the state are no longer valid today. The attraction of the Zapatistas is that by disturbing the free rein given to capital at its point of origin, they offer a form of resistance that challenges the very essence of economic rule (Holloway 2002: 87). By refusing to comply with the state and by establishing their own right to autonomy they can point to a form of contestation that combines the strategic use of the war of movement and the war of position in a potentially more successful manner than the Marxist-Leninist resistance of the past.

Lastly, the culture of resistance that the Zapatistas inspired used a new set of tools and techniques that had been alien to peasant uprisings in previous eras. The most noted here was the use of new media. As Castells has argued, the Internet became such an important actor within their strategic plan that they became known as the 'first informational guerrilla movement' (Castells 1997: 79). At what was still a relatively early stage in its development, the Internet was used to highlight the Zapatistas' humanitarian approach, raise awareness of their own plight with the Mexican state and stimulate debate about the nature of global capitalism. Yet it was perhaps the Internet's organizational potential which appeared to have the biggest effect on the nature of resistance. Not only have demonstrations been mobilized through the use of such a tool, but the manner, form and characteristic that such demonstrations might take can be organized and discussed within a virtual setting prior to the event.

There can be no doubt that the Zapatistas were a significantly influential source for the anti-neoliberal campaigns and demonstrations that followed and to a degree appear to be *the* inspirational movement that sparked such protests. Indeed, the debt owed to the Zapatistas can be clearly seen in the continued use of masks during demonstrations (Worth and Kuhling 2004). Yet, despite this, in real terms the group has not been successful in its struggle against the direction taken by the Mexican state or against NAFTA as a whole. Dialogue between the state and the EZLN took place in the form of the San Andreas Accords in 1996 and in the later meetings with Vicente Fox five years later. In the case of the former, 500 representatives and 178 organizations from Mexico's indigenous population made a set of demands for recognition of their cultural and ethnic existence (Cuninghame and Corona 1998). The unwillingness to implement these demands saw a stalemate between both sides that wasn't broken until 2001, when Fox announced he would reopen negotiations with the EZLN over their constitutional rights. This resulted in the group marching to the capital and presenting their case to Congress. The resulting proposals, however, were rejected by the Zapatistas. Instead, they continued to align with their independent '32 autonomous municipalities' within the Chiapas region.

While the Zapatistas appear to be an organization that embodies the very principles of progressive expression against the ideological might of the global economy, the reality is that they have not achieved a great deal in terms of changing the political realities of Mexican life. In addition, while the idea of self-autonomy might challenge the very common sense of the way in which political society is played out, the effectiveness of such a strategy as a sustainable long-term project is highly questionable. The idea of groups declaring independence from the state in which they reside because of opposition to policy considered to be unconstitutional is not new,[1] and the results have never led to any meaningful challenge at a higher level. More importantly, in order for such strategies to develop into a wider alternative project, they would need to explore a comprehensive plan for how such autonomy from below develops into something that actually affects and has the capability of altering state and institutional policy.

Global civil society and cosmopolitanism

More sustainable ideas for alternative economic governance have emerged through the increasing significance of global civil society. As a concept, global civil society has attracted great debate in recent years, with some suggesting that its emergence has altered the perception of the way in which states and governments choose to operate. The influence of transnational civil society has been something that has flourished within liberal societies since the campaign to end the slave trade at the beginning of the nineteenth century (David 2007). The post-Cold War environment has allowed civil society movements to become far more organized and more entrenched in global society. Non-governmental organizations (NGOs) have emerged in areas ranging from universal human rights and international justice to gender empowerment and environmentalism. As Gramsci is quick to remind us, civil society serves as the ground where ideas can win over and common sense can be constructed. Thus, in a liberal democracy it is relied upon to secure the 'hearts and minds' of popular consent (Gramsci 1971: 333) and is facilitated through different activities and in different ways. Therefore, at a global level, civil society seeks to both reinforce the general status quo and struggle against it at the same time. Indeed, the paradox of global civil society is that, to quote from one of its leading experts, it:

> includes the INGOs and the networks that are the 'tamed' successors to the new social movements of the 1970s and 1980s. It also includes the allies of transnational business who promote a free market framework at a global level. It includes a new radical anti-capitalist movement, which combines both the successors of the new social movements and the new type of labour movement. (Kaldor 2003: 108)

The idea of radical global civil society from below is that of mobilizing towards the establishment of an alternative to the free market through the setting up of NGOs that campaign for social protection from market rule. Ultimately, the objective here is to make a set of transnational networks that will create a sort of 'postmodern Prince' capable of challenging neoliberal governance and business centricity (Gill 2000). Therefore, a collection of labour movements, environmental movements, citizens' rights campaigners, developmental workers and charities have been utilized to argue for the drastic reform of global institutions, a wider form of economic and social intervention in order to reduce global inequality, and widespread welfare and labour reform to eradicate poverty and exclusion.

Funding initiatives and partnerships with UN agencies have allowed NGOs new incentives to develop greater scope and potential for radicalism, but at the same time it can be argued that they have been embedded or at least formalized in a setting which lessens the potential for radicalism. Certainly, one of the most effective critiques of global civil society along these lines has been from David Chandler. In *Constructing Global Civil Society* he argues that much that has been made of and written about the concept as an emancipating tool for change stems from elitist positions that have not come from 'below' as such, but from individual and abstract ideas. The idea that civil society is responding to abuses at an international level through the construction of NGOs is one that is debatable. What is more apparent is that NGOs have been constructed by individuals that have dominant ideas on how they would like to change the world. As such the aims of specific NGOs are determined by the will of the 'powerful, rather than the struggles of the powerless' (Chandler 2004: 107).

One example of how Chandler's critique can be tested is through the idea of cosmopolitanism. Cosmopolitanism has emerged as an alternative framework for global governance, largely from the classroom as opposed to from the 'real' world. Based on an argument that communities have shared ideas and shared morals, it argues that the nation-state system and contemporary capitalism have sought to undermine these universal principles. The post-Cold War period of globalization has produced opportunities for the state system to be transformed into a global democratic unit, with the process of economic reform and distribution being a necessary requirement (Archibugi and Held 1995; Archibugi 2003; Held and McGrew 2003). For those who advocate cosmopolitanism a clear strategy exists for global change. The moves towards global accountability and equality

can occur only through global institutions that are represented democratically. This would mean the construction of some form of global
parliament alongside a global economic polity. Cosmopolitanism has
found only lukewarm support among NGO workers and activists
associated with the anti-/alter-globalization movement. While it does
indicate a way in which global democracy can be built, it also attracts
criticisms that it is somewhat missing the point of the wider civil
campaigns. For example, the whole purpose of grassroots radicalism
was that it rejected the top-down governmental approach of con-
ventional politics. By favouring the notion of self-autonomy, groups
such as the Zapatistas have been clear in their rejection of traditional
power in favour of collective power. An alternative that primarily
bases itself upon a global form of social democracy is not one that
is going to hold much appeal for those who dismiss Western-centric
understandings of democracy. Similarly, it does not hold much appeal
for the more traditional class-based critics who favour a return to the
central principles of socialism (Callinicos 2003).

As Chandler suggests, cosmopolitanism does seem to be the general
official approach favoured by NGOs within global civil society to
counterbalance the inequalities brought about by globalization. It also
seems to be the favoured solution for critics such as Joseph Stiglitz,
who have argued that the starting point for any progressive alternative to neoliberalism has to be a democratic reform of key economic
institutions such as the World Bank and the IMF (Stiglitz 2006).
Chandler is also right to suggest that cosmopolitanism emerged from
within the minds of academics and economists and from influential
NGOs. There is also a strong argument for the idea that a global
civil society based upon cosmopolitan principles is largely a Western
construct and that NGOs in developing countries are attempting to
install such principles to fulfil their own self-proclaimed vision of
'good governance'. Yet at the same time such moves can also be seen
as essential for the building of a successful alternative hegemonic
programme. As was illustrated in the last chapter, it is the combination of ideas from traditional and organic intellectuals which forges a
successful hegemonic project, and differences and diversities logically
occur. Therefore, ideas on how the world should be transformed from
traditional intellectuals and elites can find compatibility with organic
movements from below, provided a common thread exists between
them. If the Zapatistas represent the mobilization of resistance and

cosmopolitanism represents the traditional intellectual response, then it has been the vast variety of street protest groups which have made up the organic response and have tested the common legitimacy of neoliberal rule.

The anti-globalization movements

The collection of groups and activities that have made up the protest movements have been referred to as the 'anti-globalization' movement, the 'alter-globalization' movement, the 'global justice' movement and the 'anti-capitalist' movement. The general focus of the movement was to target meetings and summits of international economic institutions.

The first place where the movement came to prominence was at the World Trade Organization's (WTO) Ministerial Conference in Seattle in 1999. NGOs, labour unions such as the AFL-CIO, pressure groups and religious groups such as Jubilee 2000 and Christian Aid joined political organizations that were rooted in anarchism, socialism and environmentalism in protesting against the potential consequences of the meeting. Perhaps what is now forgotten is that the protests emanated from opposition to the Multilateral Agreement on Investment (MAI) drafted by the OECD in the years preceding Seattle. In this the OECD sought to introduce a collection of rules based upon the mass liberalization of investment regimes and investment protection (Witherell 1995). The opposition to the move from a host of NGOs resulted in the subsequent shelving of the proposal. The belief that a version of the MAI would emerge at Seattle led to the demonstrations.

The subsequent clashes with police, the separation between the non-violent protesters or 'fluffies' and those in favour of direct action ('spikies'), slogans against corporate power, global capitalism and free trade became commonplace. Subsequent protests occurred during the World Bank–IMF meeting in Washington, DC, in 2000, in Montreal and Quebec during the G7 and the Summit of the Americas in 2000/01 and at the G8 in Genoa, where the clashes between the authorities and protesters resulted in the death of a young activist. In addition to this were the annual May Day protests in London, where situationism, and, to borrow from Bakhtin, the carnival of protest, came alive, with groups such as Reclaim the Streets, Critical Mass and the Wombles[2] mixing protest with art, creativity and humour. At first, the groups were identified by critics as being both 'anti-progressive' and 'anti-trade' in nature, and were criticized by neoliberal and Keynesian economists alike for the perception that they were anti-trade (Krugman 1999). The retort from protesters was that they were only anti-free-trade in that the point of entry favours advanced economies and companies. This led to a growth in ethical fair trade, which ironically has been taken up by certain companies as a new profit-making initiative.

Since the heyday of the anti-globalization street protests in the aftermath of the Seattle conference, such resistance has continued, but has often manifested itself in different ways. Certain events, such as the G8 Gleneagles Summit in Edinburgh in 2005, attracted a huge gathering that placed celebrity campaigners alongside – and often against – the now established hardened street protesters.[3] More prominently, protests have been more spontaneous in recent years, and have largely followed the implementation of specific policy – national or international – without altering the overriding nature or character of previous campaigns. The various groups that made up the movements against global organizations in the period between 1999 and 2003 were also involved in the similar anti-war demonstrations from 2003. Here, in tandem with the historical development of the neoliberal order that I demonstrated in Chapter 1, the rhetoric of campaigns was altered to include criticisms of 'imperialism' and to press for for an 'anti-imperialist world'.

By 2008, many critics and mainstream news agencies had written off what they still referred to at the time as the 'anti-globalization' movement. Many popular academics had been arguing for a long time that the campaigns lacked an overall objective or that the overall results of free markets and private investment had led to a decrease in absolute poverty (Bhagwati 2004; Friedman 2005; Wolf 2004). In the light of the financial crisis, the protest movements seemed at first to revert to national concerns. However, the growth in 2011 of the Occupy movement has placed them back into the spotlight. Now predominantly seen as 'anti-capitalist', the Occupy movement has continued where 'anti-globalization' or 'global justice' movements had left off. Organized through the Internet and new media, the Occupy movement seeks to use public spaces to protest against the structure and appearance of global capitalism. By the end of 2011 camps or protest sites had been set up in around three thousand towns and cities worldwide. The most notable camps have been set up in public areas outside financial companies in key urban areas. This is a classic situationist tactic. By protesting in areas that are close to places of symbolic power, demonstrators can both attract attention to their cause and introduce confusion over whether they have a right to occupy public areas in such a manner. In London, for example, it was ruled that the area outside the stock exchange was privately owned, resulting in the movement relocating to outside St Paul's Cathedral (another well-known landmark). In Washington, DC, and Los Angeles, the movement has attracted a confused response from authorities, with certain areas deemed acceptable and others unacceptable, leading to activist arrests. In continental Europe, there were also stark differences in the manner of protest. While in Germany peaceful protests were commonplace in key financial cities such as Berlin and Frankfurt, violent demonstrations erupted in crisis-torn Italy.

The Occupy movement can claim that it is following the strategy of the Zapatistas in the sense of reclaiming areas for self-autonomy. However, it owes its development to the Canadian protest movement Adbusters. Well versed in the traditions of situationism, Adbusters became a key player in the subversion of popular advertisement campaigns in order to expose the contradictions that exist within them (for example, replacing Nike's 'Just do it' with 'Just screw it' and 'Absolut Vodka' with 'Absolut Nonsense' – see Worth and Kuhling 2004). The global ambitions of Adbusters' previous campaigning led to them inspiring the Occupy Wall Street movement, which was then ready to branch out. The Occupy Wall Street campaign can rightly be seen as the most significant in terms of its impact and popular appeal, and the movement has spread truly globally, with campaigns reaching as far as Manila, Ulan Bator, Johannesburg and, aided by the Arab Spring uprisings, to Tunis and Cairo. This has also answered previous criticisms that the mass protest movement was essentially a Western-centric project (Shipman 2002).

The anti-globalization/anti-capitalist movement has led to widespread protest to which leaders and prominent figures in the global economy have had to respond. While Seattle may have brought condemnation from some leaders, the Occupy movement has generally attracted sympathy from world leaders. Despite this, the aims and objectives of the movements still appear woolly and imprecise at best. Despite broad support for campaigns such as the Robin Hood tax and notions such as wealth redistribution, the ideas of the campaign at this very early stage appear rather ambiguous.

The World Social Forum

The World Social Forum (WSF) was founded as a means of bringing together NGOs, social movements and indigenous groups in order to combine ideas and strategies to pursue a more just world. It was set up to coincide with the annual World Economic Forum in Davos under the working framework that 'Another world is possible'. Set up by those associated with Pôrto Alegre's branch of the Partido dos Trabalhadores (Workers' Party, abbreviated as PT), it sought to forge a set of alternative proposals to the hegemony of neoliberalism, based upon the principles of 'open space'. This allows for the discussion and engagement of specific ideas and suggestions, without adhering to dominant mandates. Since its inception in 2001, the WSF has been quick to realize the importance of creating regional forums so as to present a wider devolved umbrella movement. As such, the European Social Forum, the Asian Social Forum, the Boston Social Forum and then later the African Social Forum offered a space where regionally specific issues could be voiced.

The nature of this 'open space' is defined in the WSF's charter, which explicitly states that a) it is a process whereby the building of alternatives cannot be reduced to the events supporting it; b) no one can presume to speak for the forum as a whole; and c) that it relies upon a series of exchanges in order to seek to forge greater links and mutual recognition between globally diverse groups and individuals (WSF 2007). For some, the WSF had the foundations to build a counter-hegemonic movement to rival and challenge any developments at Davos. They argue that despite coming from diverse parts, the WSF can use the arena of open space to create a general coherence that can be articulated as an alternative form of common sense (Fisher and Ponniah 2003). In this way some form of unified position can be formed that would accord with the metaphor of Stephen Gill's postmodern Prince, which he called for in the aftermath of Seattle (Gill 2000).[4]

The Forum's successful period could be seen as being between the years 2004 and 2007. During this time it moved location from Pôrto Alegre (2001–03) to Mumbai (2004) and back (2005), before choosing multiple sites for 2006 (Caracas, Bamako and Karachi).

These attracted significant crowds that reached well over 100,000 for 2004, with estimates at Pôrto Alegre the following year being as high as 155,000. At the Polycentric Forum in 2006 attendance was estimated to be in excess of this level collectively, and it was this process which led to the establishment of the Bamako Appeal, which established that the WSF should be seen as a collective yet diverse project of socialism and anti-imperialism. However, by the time the Forum reached Nairobi in 2007 criticisms of the process were only too evident. The spiritual base of Pôrto Alegre as a venue became untenable when the PT party began to lose influence in the city and the new mayor dismissed the Forum as an 'ideological Disneyland'. This meant that permanent alternative venues were needed to host future forums. Nairobi was hailed as one which would represent a new dawn for the Forum as it was to centre on Africa for the first time. Yet it was at Nairobi that clashes between participants became more evident.

First, it appeared that there was an insider/outsider feel to the Forum that was represented at every level. Several participants were not allowed into the arena for cost reasons and promptly set up alternative gatherings elsewhere (TerraViva 2007). The Forum's activities placed Western NGOs and academics in the main localities within the arena, while local groups were placed in the peripheral areas. This also mirrored the catering of the Forum, which was divided between the well-established companies that operated inside the arena (including one that was owned by the Kenyan internal security minister) and the self-contained outlets outside. Secondly, there was a feeling that the Forum was becoming increasingly unrepresentative and directionless. Finally, there was a sense that activities such as the slum visit that took place were both patronizing and insensitive.

All this reflects a broader charge of elitism that had been a growing feature of criticism for some time. The make-up of the organizing committee and the general participants has long been dominated by academics and NGO activists with a high level of education (Sousa Santos 2006). The activities themselves have ranged from addresses that would have been better suited to an academic conference to the advertisement of particular activities from NGOs. As has been argued by some, using an open-space formula exacerbates the situation whereby the more privileged gain more access (Biagiotti 2004). Such developments have indeed been noted by prominent activists such as

Naomi Klein, who pointed to the dangers of such forums resulting in brand wars between NGOs (Klein 2003).

The charge of elitism should not just be reserved for NGO policy-makers and academics, however. Despite being an apolitical body, the Forum has been attended by many politicians and representatives of political parties who have used it for political advantage. The PT and Brazil's former president Lula received considerable backing from the WSF and have, in turn, used it to promote their political agenda. Chávez has gone farther, using the forums in part to mobilize popular and populist support. This was most evident in the Belém forum of 2009, where the five South American left leaders (Lula, Morales, Chávez, Correa and Lugo) shared a platform to highlight the fact that they had been right about the capitalism system after all. This was despite the fact that many had previously been keen participants at the World Economic Forum.

Despite these charges made against the World Social Forum, it has continued to exist as an event where alternative ideas and strategies can be voiced. At Dakar in 2011 it attracted 75,000 participants, which showed an increase over those that attended at the previous African event (an estimated 65,000 at Nairobi). Aided by the start of the 'Arab Spring' protests, the event brought a new incentive for democratic mobilization and fresh optimism that the forums can continue to expand at both regional and global level to seek new areas of convergence. For its supporters, this demonstrates the ability of the process to attract movements from all parts of the globe, irrespective of the stage of their economic development or cultural form. It also shows that the system of open space is effective as it allows for a continuing exchange of new ideas and is geared towards an inclusivity that adapts to new concepts and developments.

Despite this it would be wrong to assume that the WSF has been a success. For all the numbers that have participated and the new ground made, it is as far away from realizing its dream of another world as ever before. The open-space formula instigated by the WSF remains highly ambiguous, highly contradictory and ultimately unworkable as a strategy. Perhaps the best indication of this is found in points 6 and 7 of the charter. Point 6 states that:

> The participants ... shall not be called to take decisions as a body, whether by vote or accumulation, on declarations or proposals for

action that would commit all, or the majority of them, and that purpose to be taken as establishing positions of the Forum as a body. It thus does not constitute a locus of power to be disputed by the participants in its meetings, nor does it intend to constitute the only option for interrelation and action by the organisations and movements that participate in it. (WSF 2007: 17)

This is followed by point 7, which states that:

Nonetheless, organisations or groups of organisations that participate in the Forum's meetings must be assured the right, during such meetings, to deliberate on declarations or actions they might decide on, whether singly or in coordination with other participants. (Ibid.: 17)

This in itself provides a confusing model of how decision-making powers are allocated, apart from suggesting that organizations might want to coordinate in making declarations that could lead to greater cooperation. Even if the principle of open space is geared towards establishing this sort of dialogue, there have been no firm proposals to emerge from these interactions to suggest that a coherent alternative is forthcoming. If the purpose of the WSF was to produce the space for global civil society, traditional and organic intellectuals and activists from below to sow the seeds of such an alternative, as proponents have argued (Fisher and Ponniah 2003), then it has failed in its task.

Not only have the WSF and its regional counterparts been unable to offer any significant alternative to the process of global governance, they have remained plagued by the charge of elitism. Participants have not been able to shake off the tag of 'the privileged enlightened few', whose honourable ideals largely remain detached from political reality. As I have argued with Karen Buckley elsewhere, the World Social Forum perhaps best represents the criticisms that David Chandler has made regarding global civil society (Chandler 2004, 2007; Worth and Buckley 2009). Too often the ideals of the forums seem to be constructed by individuals and organizations, who imagine an alternative world through the deployment of complex theories and speak on behalf of the subaltern (Worth and Buckley 2009: 659). The inability to separate the Forum from either a gathering of NGOs competing for attention or an academic conference seems to remain a permanent problem.

This is not to say that there have been no positives to have come from the events that have been staged by the respective social forums. The forums have, for example, developed community empowerment and education groups that have been led by local communities, which have provided civic advice on certain customs (such as gender inequalities, female circumcision, etc.). Yet, in terms of providing a potential base to bring together the disparate elements of the alter-globalization movement and to build an alternative world, the WSF has fallen short. Even during the 2009 and 2011 forums, with the backdrop of the financial crisis and the difficult WEFs that coincided with them, no concrete alternatives were tabled to challenge global capitalism. This would suggest that perhaps its time as a potential agent of change has passed.

The political left

If the WSF might have offered a route towards building a hegemonic base to challenge neoliberalism, then what of traditional party mobilization? As stated above, one of the problems of the WSF was that its own ideals did not seem to captivate electorates across the world. Despite the rise in civil societal resistance and in social protests, there has not been a significant swing to left-progressive political parties in the last few decades. Indeed, while much of the anti-globalization activity was a response to the 'third-way' rhetorical turn of the mainstream left, this has not been reflected through the ballot box. Alternative left parties have fared poorly, with a lack of significant breakthroughs being made in terms of political representation. One of the more notable observations to be made during the fallout from the financial crisis was that the left did not have much of a response. In much of Europe the failure of the left at the polls – including in social democratic strongholds such as Sweden – reflected the lack of direction it had collectively (Worth 2012).

The exception to this trend was of course South America. The electoral success of the left and the emergence of Chávez, Morales, Lula and his successor Dilma Rousseff have put the continent at the forefront of left-wing revivalism in global politics. Here two points remain of interest, however. First, while there has been a shift to the left and towards confronting neoliberal policies in the aftermath of the debt crisis, there are doubts as to whether public consciousness shows a similar trend. Quantitative studies on public attitudes to liberty, tolerance and democracy have placed Latin America collectively to the right of global attitudes as a whole, with Venezuela averaging to the right within the whole region. Here, attitudes that are generally favoured by the left (or at least the post-Soviet left) are not evident across the region as a whole, despite the move to the left at the electoral level (Seligson 2006). What has emerged instead is an increase in populism and acceptance of the idea of a strong form of leadership. The popular rejection of Americanism and of the idea of neoliberalism from above has played to this populism. At the same time, as I outlined above, the mobilization of support that both the PT and Chávez achieved at the WSF in Pôrto Alegre, Belém and Caracas contributed to this process.[5]

Secondly, it remains questionable what form the left is actually taking in the region. This goes beyond the arguments by Castaneda that two lefts are emerging that take their cue either from the Perón/Chávez brand of anti-Americanism or the Lula/PT vision of cosmopolitan solidarity (Castaneda 2006). For example, the historical and political experiences of an energy-rich state such as Venezuela support claims that popular authoritarian leaderships emerge from the so-called 'resource curse' (Ross 1999). Therefore, rather than adopting strong leadership in order to create a socialist response to aggressive neoliberalism, Chávez is merely playing out the role of the autocrat protecting his resources from outsiders. This differs from the role of Morales in Bolivia, who has engaged in a number of 'eclectic' ideas that range from the land movement to the US-backed neoliberal initiative (Harten 2011; Petras 2007: 197–200). Bolivia's status as an agrarian HIPC (heavily indebted poor country) sets it apart from other countries in the region, but, in terms of idealistic rhetoric, Morales's own credentials as a socialist ideologist far outstripped those of any of his close contemporaries. The 'left turn' undertaken by Chile and Brazil took an altogether different route. In Chile, the spectre of Pinochet was to haunt domestic politics long after his demise. The election of Michelle Bachelet provided a way of cushioning the aggressive stance of the 1970s and 1980s. In Brazil, the positions taken by Lula and Rousseff have, to a certain extent, followed the agenda of Fernando Cardoso's third-way programme that preceded them.

This does suggest that there are not one but many variants of the left in Latin America. Some are closer to the authoritarian-populism top-down model that seems to border on protectionism, while some have stressed a form of cosmopolitanism. There are also distinct differences over whether a new form of politics is actually emerging out of Latin America that could challenge the dominant positions taken by parties in the West. In spite of the rhetoric of anti-imperialism and anti-neoliberalism, many regional specialists have argued that, rather than searching for anti-systemic solutions, the left have generally argued for better management of market economies (Panizza 2005). Therefore the full extent of the radicalism of the new South American left, especially in terms of its ability to mount a counter-hegemonic challenge, is questionable at present.

What of the political left outside of Latin America? In Europe some limited developments have been made to suggest that a form of alternative programme might be forthcoming. For example, the rise of Die Linke (the Left) in recent elections in Germany has suggested that some sort of alternative project might emerge to challenge the traditional centre-left. Established in 2007, Die Linke is a combination of a number of parties and organizations that include the former ruling Eastern European Party and those that emerged in protest against the route taken by the Social Democratic Party. It includes former finance minister Oskar Lafontaine and generally favours a Keynesian approach to immediate economic management and the reform of global economic institutions, and also adopts a pro-European approach to internationalism and integration. Its main breakthrough as an electoral force came in the 2009 Bundestag elections when it picked up nearly 12 per cent of the overall vote.

The marginal success for the left in Germany is not one that has been replicated in other parts of Europe. While there has been recent success for the United Left in Spain, this was overshadowed by the swing from the centre-left to the centre-right in light of the financial crisis. Other areas of the Eurozone that have been hit by the crisis (the so-called PIGS or PIIGS states) have not generally seen a rise in the success of alternative parties. The one exception to this could be Greece, where extreme austerity measures together with a series of economic crises saw the rise of Syriza, a left-wing umbrella movement that sought to reject any conditionality placed upon bailouts from the European Central Bank (ECB). The failure of Syriza to form a stable government following the elections of May 2012 led to a further election the following month, after which a pro-austerity government was formed. In general, however, when a ruling party has been punished by the electorate, it has often been due to their mismanagement of the economy, rather than any shift in political consciousness (as witnessed in the parliamentary elections in Ireland in 2011). This has also been reflected in the European Parliament's 'left' group – the European United Left-Nordic Green Left (GUE/NGL), who themselves make up a strange brand of socialists, Trotskyists, communist parties and 'left' nationalist parties, such as Ireland's Sinn Fein. Again, while they adopt the slogan from the European Social Forum ('Another Europe is possible'), the parties differ quite considerably in their view of the manner in which this should happen, with traditional national-first socialist parties mixing uneasily with internationalists.

In other parts of the world there is relatively little to suggest that an alternative hegemonic project from the left is being nurtured through party politics. There have been relatively few socialist-based parties to emerge since the decline of the Marxist-Leninist dogma. Those that have retained the principles have either been key players in the global economy themselves or have used them in a manner that has involved a return to twentieth-century forms of resistance. In the case of the former, the Chinese Communist Party might yet have a significant say in determining the future of neoliberalism, but this will not be in the form of any globalist cosmopolitan vision (see Chapter 7). Likewise, the various Maoist resurgences in India and Nepal might be of wider interest to us when looking at the stability of the Indian state, but the Naxalite 'struggles' draw from experiences of the twentieth century and certainly do not offer anything other than ideas that borrow from the violent insurgencies and solutions of the past. This has also been the case in the former areas of the Soviet Union, where fading communist parties have transformed into nationalist entities, embraced new forms of populism or have just gone into decline.[6]

One of the outcomes of the regional social forums is that they have served as a means of facilitating coherence for parties. Some have argued that, at the Mumbai Forum in 2004, the disparate parts of the Indian left came together. This included pitting Maoist revolutionaries alongside Gandhi-inspired organizations, which prompted observations that the left, often fragmented by ideology and regionally divided, would be transformed as a result (Leite 2005: 147–9). However, the Forum has not been able to produce any long-term convergence, with Maoist insurgency increasing since the formation of the Maoist Communist Party towards the end of 2004. This and its subsequent abolition by the state have continued to drive a wedge between the left as a whole, which grassroots organizations have been unable to prevent.

Conclusion: any sign of the postmodern Prince?

This chapter has assessed the nature, strength and content of groups and organizations that might be considered as offering a socially progressive and internationalist challenge on which an alternative hegemonic project can be based. What has been evident is that since the end of the Cold War the solutions put forward have drastically differed from either the Marxism-Leninism of the Soviet era or parliamentary forms that were popular in western Europe. Instead, there is a recognition that globalization brings with it a potential to transform the current system and build another world. This is obviously reflected in the WSF's 'Another world is possible' slogan. The premise is that civil society will build solidarity through networks and that this will provide a space where actions and ideas can be deployed. One favoured alternative has been to follow the self-autonomy that had been practised by the Zapatistas in response to the Mexican state, so as to contest capitalism at its first point of interaction. How this might look on the broader scale is difficult to say; such a solution might work as a form of dissent, but how would it work as a project of transformation?

The movements that have come under the global justice or alter-globalization umbrella have certainly highlighted the problems and shortcomings of the contemporary form of capitalism, and to this extent have managed to question the legitimacy of neoliberalism. Just how far this has gone in building a coherent internationalist or globalist alternative is far more debatable. Many of the campaigns that have come from civil society have been from groups that would be considered as 'middle-class' (Chase-Dunn and Reese 2007), and electoral developments have shown that parties that represent such ideas for change have not made any major breakthrough. In regions such as South America, where the left has been regarded as a counter-hegemony force, the realities are not as clear cut. Yet, as this chapter has shown, the main problem has been that the form and content of the new just world that is imagined are not clear. Strategies (including forms of self-autonomy) have been aired, but most have been vague in their arguments and have been considered unrealistic by those in power. The World Social Forum's policy of open space has, if anything, made these disparities more notable. Certain ideas such as a global currency transaction tax (or Tobin tax) and the Robin Hood tax have been discussed, as indeed they were within mainstream politics back in 2007. The type of democratic accountability, the reform of global governance and the transformation of neoliberalism required will all need greater clarity for a counter-hegemonic project to succeed. In addition, greater cohesion is needed between different parts of society for it to gain popular appeal.

4 | NATIONALIST AND EXCEPTIONALIST RESPONSES

We are the angry mob, we read the papers everyday. We like who we like, we hate who we hate. But we're also easily swayed (Kaiser Chiefs, 2007)

Globalization is often understood as being a process that has transformed existing societies in such a manner that it has rendered previous forms of governance redundant (Camilleri and Falk 1992) and has altered the previous conception about the nature of identity and the role of the nation-state (Croucher 2004). It has also led to a competing number of interpretations of the manner in which globalization has come about. Nationalist, populist and reactionary responses to the development of globalization have generally been the result of a conviction that globalism is a process that seeks to destroy the appearance and culture of the nation-state and as such threatens the very fabric of national life. Often, the expressions of these reactions, especially in their most extreme form, are channelled through narratives that blame certain social groups and intellectual traditions for its development.

The pursuit of nationalism as a counter to globalism is not surprising. Unlike cosmopolitan-based solutions to global capitalism, nationalism is a position that can claim to be the only true opponent of globalism (Mudde 2007: 184). It can mobilize support through the tried and tested alliance with the nation-state and its cultural forms of exceptionalism. As a concept, nationalism has long been an ideology that has attracted all sides of political life, with nativism – the belief that a country belongs to a specific national race – and racial superiority often associated with the right, playing off against national liberation movements that have traditionally been associated with the left. Nationalism also plays a significant practical role in the running and functioning of specific nation-states, the concept itself being one which is employed in specific instances for specific purposes (Smith 1995). Even when comparative western European political

NATIONALIST AND EXCEPTIONALIST RESPONSES | 73

scientists draw up the distinctions between what they would consider 'nationalist' or 'ethno-nationalist' parties (such as the Scottish, Welsh and Catalan national parties) and the populist radical right, their criteria often throw up anomalies. The Flemish Vlaams Belang Party (formerly Vlaams Bloc) is a regionalist-national party that fits more easily into the category of the populist right, while Ireland's Sinn Fein has all the hallmarks of the latter, but considers itself and acts within Europe's leftist faction (O'Malley 2008; Mudde 2007: 52–3).[1]

Nationalism therefore represents one specific and convenient way of mobilizing popular reaction against globalization. Yet, the nationalism that is articulated is one that is understood as an antidote to globalism. Indeed, globalism brings with it a number of social developments such as immigration that are damaging to the national character. There are a number of other characteristics about this specific type of resistance. First, many groups or organizations that are associated with populism or the radical right are not necessarily against neoliberal economics. Indeed, many far-right political parties in Europe came to embrace the neoliberal radicalism of the free market as a means of attacking the 'welfare-corporatist' consensus of social and Christian democracy. In addition, many associated with the American anti-globalist right emerged through the original premise of low tax and greater economic freedom. These economic positions have often changed or been compromised, however, as strategies have been reworked to tackle the main enemies at large for such groups – multiculturalism and the dissolution of national sovereignty in favour of some form of supranational or world state.

Secondly, many reactionary responses to the current order pinpoint certain individuals or a certain social group or racial social group which they believe to be responsible for eroding their respective ways of life. This can take the form of narratives that have been constructed in order to argue that globalism has been planned by certain groups in an undemocratic and unpatriotic way in order for them to construct a master plan that will benefit them. This type of 'reasoning' is based upon what are commonly called 'conspiracy theories', namely a belief that certain privileged individuals have constructed agreements against the will of the people. In addition, this is done against the tenor of popular opinion and seeks to undermine the values that bind communities together, through the use of propaganda and trickery.

The nature of conspiracy

Conspiracies have been used in a variety of different ways and have been applied to understand government cover-ups, planned assassination of individuals, various epidemics and historical events. In terms of using conspiracy theory in order to show how global events have been shaped by a specific section of society, we can use Adolf Hitler's *Mein Kampf* as an example. In this he identifies Marxism and International Jewry as two forces that have sought to undermine the Aryan race and the Germanic nation. He also outlines his ten-stage schema of how the Jewish race asserts power and influence over the nation. Here, 'the Jew' is seen as an outsider, who slowly enters and manipulates society for his own gain. He moves from a position as a trader to one where he controls and dominates the financial workings of society, before destroying it with a destruction ideology (that of Marxism) (Hitler 1992: 280–96). The extreme manner in which Hitler blames a race for the way in which society is ordered demonstrates the nature of the scapegoat within the mind of the conspiracy theorist. The scapegoat can represent a set of individuals, a race or a specific political organization. Generally speaking, in terms of the latter, the left is the most likely to be cast in this role, yet much of the emerging European far right has laid blame on the 'liberal elite' that dominates centre politics. However, quite often the 'Marxist' left and 'liberal' centre or centre-right emerge as one large group responsible for societal ills, either by facilitating dangerous ideologies or being too weak to confront them.

As globalism represents the contemporary ideological danger to society, it is here that conspiracies are built. Both Mark Rupert and Manuel Castells have made detailed studies of the emergence in the 1990s of far-right anti-globalization protectionism in the USA (Rupert 2000: 94–118; Castells 1997: 84–97). For them, conspiracy is based upon a belief that a group of individuals is attempting to construct an undemocratic form of global governance whereby a global dictatorship will emerge. This narrative has largely emerged since the end of the Cold War and coincided with George Bush Snr's proclamation of a 'New World Order' in the aftermath of the first Gulf War. Bush was a renowned target for conspiracy theorists owing to his previous involvement with the CIA as the Director of Central Intelligence in the 1970s. The New World Order suddenly became a term that was used to describe a grand pact involving an elite collection of leading figures that have sought to build a secret world.

The first major source of this new type of conspiracy was the televangelist Pat Robertson, whose book *The New World Order* was to become a reference point for future conspiracy theorists. Largely borrowing from controversial figures in the past who had previously passed themselves off as traditional intellectuals for far-right organizations,[2] the book argues that a number of secret organizations have emerged throughout history that are committed to overthrowing civilization as they understand it in return for a new undemocratic 'world order'. The main areas of American civilization which Robertson believes to be under threat are private property, individual liberty and religion (or, in his case, the Christian Church) (Robertson 1991). Secret organizations were set up that planned ways in which this operation could be carried out, and subsequent governments have been manipulated by individuals who have had links to or have been active members of such groups. Robertson's book seemed to unleash a thriving body of conspiracy theorists who have gained in popularity owing to widening forms of communication. Indeed, the Internet has been a notorious haven, allowing both conspiracy theories to flourish and conspiracy theorists themselves to develop their 'arguments' and 'research'.

Conspiracy theories have often drawn from a wider body of traditions and have not necessarily always been seen as a product of the populist right. For example, the much-referred-to 9/11 conspiracy theories have often been seen as attracting just as much interest from the left as they do from the right. Of particular reference here is the work of popular leftists such as Noam Chomsky. Chomsky attracted accusations that his own claims of how power operated drew more from conspiracy theory than from his own form of institutional analysis. This is a charge that became prominent during his filming of *Manufacturing Consent* and the development of his 'propaganda model' on the mass media that he developed with Edward Herman (Chomsky 1996; Herman and Chomsky 1998). In light of his criticisms of American power post-9/11, he made efforts to distance himself from conspiracy theories that had emerged which suggested the attacks on the Twin Towers were an 'inside job', but in doing so opened himself up to fresh criticisms by suggesting that he wouldn't be shocked if the Bush administration itself had been feeding such conspiracies (Chomsky 2007). However, what tends to distinguish the analytical claims of the left (however crude and deterministic they might tend to be) from populist forms of conspiracy is that while they are based on what might be seen as structural, positional or material concerns with the real world, the latter are driven by abstract narratives. What unites New World Order theorists is the belief that the post-Cold War proclamation by George Bush was a message to imply that a new attempt was under way on the part of this secret elite to plot world domination.

If conspiracy is used as the narrative behind the new fear of globalism, then who are the new actors behind these conspiracies? In general terms these range from the far fetched to the downright ridiculous, but many point to the Freemasons and events from the nineteenth century as their historical departure point. Freemasons may have provided the means and exhibited sufficient secrecy for a conspiracy to gather momentum, but families such as the Rothschilds and the Rockefellers were the early prominent figures. Such banking families were to construct international banking in such a manner that it would 'control money supply, manipulate the macro-economy and facilitate the creation of credit-money and the expansion of private and public debt' (Rupert 2000: 99). This in turn would lead to organizations such as the Bilderberg group, later the Trilateral Commission, which would have huge significance for the ways in which UN bodies such as the World Bank were run.

Since the end of the Cold War, which led to the formation of the New World Order, some, such as those prominently concerned with protecting the American way and whom Mark Rupert's work concentrates on, have suggested that globalism has replaced Marxism as the new avenue through which conspirators are building a world government. While before, such critics claimed that Bolshevism was bankrolled by the elites to facilitate one mechanism to bring about the destruction of American civil society, now they began to argue that this destruction would be maintained through international governmental structures such as the UN (ibid.: 99–100). Others have based their claims on wider forms of paranoia, which are directed more at the transnational nature and purpose of the ruling elites themselves. These have included prophecies of doom, from religious preachers foreseeing different forms of doomsday and the forthcoming fight between good and evil,[3] to a belief that a new Judaic power elite is being constructed and has been mobilized since the foundation of the Israeli state, and finally that the New World Order is being controlled by a 'reptilian race' that has appeared in the form of governing human families.[4]

Again, this is not to say that the left themselves have not ignored accounts that look at similar institutions when analysing the significance of modern capitalism. For example, Kees van der Pijl's classic studies on the formation of the transnational capitalist class system looks at how organizations such as the Bilderberg group managed to forge linkages between individuals and their capital interests in different parts of the world, and indeed how groups such as the Freemasons socially facilitated such a process (Van der Pijl 1998). Yet conspiracy theorists have taken this process and supplied it with a narrative that makes all sorts of wild and peculiar claims and accusations. Of particular interest is how individuals have supposedly devised secret plans that allow them to manipulate all forms of government for their own aims. It is here that prejudices are played out and fear and hatred are expressed towards certain groups whom the globalists are perceived to support within society. It is also from here that populist opinions and strategies for alternative futures are formed.

The American Patriots From 1992 until the emergence of the Bush administration at the turn of the twenty-first century, great emphasis was placed on the significance of a new form of resistance within the USA to the post-Cold War era and the New World Order (Castells 1997: 84–97; Rupert 2000: 102–10; Worth 2002: 307–9; Steger 2005: 95–106). The Waco massacre in 1993, during which federal agents attacked and killed members of a religious sect over alleged illegal activities, added to the conspiracy that the FBI was part of a larger governmental plot to erode the American way of life and led to a succession of organizations that sought to resist what they saw as changes imposed from above. The Timothy McVeigh-led assault on the FBI buildings in Oklahoma unleashed a whole collection of claims and counter-claims on the nature of federal power in the USA and the extent to which authorities would go to conspire towards its growth and consolidation. As a result, the 1990s saw a growth in groups geared towards protecting the rights of Americans from governmental and globalist influences. The establishment of local militia, the repoliticization of the gun lobby and the resurgence of civil and religious groups of all guises occurred in order to protect and strengthen constitutional rights. The development of new media also allowed groups such as the John Birch Society and the Liberty Lobby to find new support for their populist protection of American society. Such organizations have long outlined external threats to American society that come from socialist, communist, Judaic and Islamic influences, and from German, Israeli, Slavic and (through the Larouche movement) British traditions. Dangerous individuals have included Marx, Lenin, Stalin, Hitler and Keynes, who have all, in different ways, aimed to promote ideologies that threaten the American constitution.

In general terms, American Patriots have been opposed to organizations such as NAFTA and the WTO and have argued that these organizations have sought to erode the unique form of civil society and governance that the USA was founded upon. The emergence and relative success of Ross Perot in the 1992 presidential election on an economic nationalist platform that also favoured huge federal spending cuts and the subsequent formation of the Reform Party provided a platform whereby greater support could be generated. His successor Pat Buchanan may not have gained the appeal and support that Perot's earlier campaigns had in terms of votes,[5] but in the environment at the time in which the nature of free trade was being debated, Buchanan's protectionist position was quite clear:

> What is Economic Nationalism? Is it some right-wing or radical idea? By no means. Economic nationalism was the idea and cause that brought Washington, Hamilton and Madison to Philadelphia. These men dreamed of creating here in America the greatest free market on earth, by eliminating all internal barriers to trade among the 13 states, and taxing imports to finance the turnpikes and canals of the new nation and end America's dependence on Europe. It was called the American System. (Buchanan 1998)

Support for this position consolidated during the Clinton years, but tailed off during the George W. Bush administration and the populism that surrounded the second Gulf War. Since the end of the Bush administration, the failure of the War on Terror to reach a viable conclusion and the global financial crisis have seen a re-emergence of these positions, but from a wider variety of organizations. The Reform Party might distance itself from the Tea Party movement (Choate 2010), but owing to the latter's success and the prominence of other minor organizations such as the Libertarian Party, its appeal has waned in recent years.

The explicit pursuit of protectionism and of an alternative form of political economy was deeply rooted within the Perot/Buchanan philosophy. Other concerns such as immigration, federal spending (or 'big government') and the reform of the Federal Reserve have been taken up and placed to the fore by the Tea Party. In addition, they have appealed to Patriots and conspiracy theorists alike without having to resort to a clear move to protectionism. The main arguments of the 1990s, for example, seemed to stem from the belief that the international actors and institutions were being set up to threaten the American constitution and the rejection of such institutions in favour of national alternatives seemed the most pressing objective. This favoured a rejection of the neoliberal economy and a return to an era of mercantilism. Despite the financial crisis and the election of Obama, the same conspiracies and bugbears remain, but the proposed solutions have often been slightly different. Ron Paul, the new darling of the libertarian right and at the time of writing gaining significant – but ultimately not critical – support for the Republican presidential nomination, has taken an extreme reading of Hayek in order to redress constitutional rights and the ending of federal power in the USA (Paul 2008). His main arguments are that institutional organizations have not led to free trade or provided free markets, but have resulted in managed forms of state-led corporatism. For him, therefore, an end to political bureaucracy and regulation can provide the impetus for the safeguarding of the American constitution and produce the Hayekian eldorado that the advisers of Thatcher and Reagan were keen to develop two decades before. Paul's wooing of the ultra-conservative John Birch Society has appealed to those in fear of the New World Order as he promises an end to formal bureaucratic governance.

The development and position of the Patriot movement in the USA have illustrated a common problem that national-populists have in framing an alternative. As stated in the introduction, many of the concerns that some positions have are over the social and political consequences of globalism, rather than with the general ideology of neoliberalism. If this appears evident within Europe, then it is also true within the USA, where such positions are generally still supportive of Reagan's form of populism in the 1980s. Therefore, no matter how absurd and aggressive the grand narratives that accompany claims from American Patriot movements, their main ideology can still be contained in a manner that does not necessarily threaten the fundamental appearance of the contemporary world order.

Slavic mythology In 1993, in the aftermath of the collapse of the USSR, President Yeltsin decided to dissolve parliament in an attempt to instigate a new post-Soviet constitution. This was the result of a succession of conflicts between Yeltsin and the Congress of People's Deputies, founded in 1989, over, among other things, the nature of economic reform, which had started so disastrously the previous year with the economic shock doctrine and price liberalization. The conflict reached its climax when a collection of communists and nationalists committed to reclaiming the old Supreme Soviet clashed with the Yeltsin-backed army, resulting in the deaths of nearly two hundred people. What was evident here was that the activists protesting against Yeltsin were representative of all ages of Russian society, and that there was a significantly large collection of nationalist and hard-line communist groups taking part in the demonstrations. This was reflected in popular support when, by the time the new elections were called, the combined vote for nationalist and communist forces approached 40 per cent of the popular vote.

The roots in nationalist support could be seen back in the glasnost era of Gorbachev, when an organization known as Pamyat (memory) began to critique Marxism-Leninism as a familiar and predictable Zionist–Masonic conspiracy and gained momentum as an organization geared towards upholding the protection of Russian cultural heritage (Cox and Shearman 2000; Worth 2005: 199–220). By the time Yeltsin had succeeded Gorbachev and had dismantled the Soviet Union, the nationalist revival in Russia had reached new heights with the onset of a variety of 'nationalist' and 'pan-Slavic' groups emerging to contest any attempt to Westernize the Russian state and race (Verkhovsky 2000; Shnirelman 1998). The most obvious was Vladimir Zhirinovsky's ultra-nationalist party (the contradictorily named Liberal Democratic Party of Russia, LDPR), which took 23 per cent of the vote in 1993.

The pan-Slavic movement partly emerged from a conviction that the Slavic nations differ from the Western or European states in both their cultural and political expression. Drawing from the writings of the nineteenth-century romantic nationalist Nikolai Danilevskii, Slavism was seen as a tradition that drew upon autocracy, paternalism and economic protectionism. As a reaction against the British-led liberal capitalist trading system at the time, pan-Slavism was designed to institute an alternative ethnic, cultural and geopolitical regime to those in Europe. The rebirth of such positions in post-Soviet Russia saw an aggressive mobilization against 'Americanism' and support for much-maligned leaders such as Slobodan Milosevic. Milosevic's ethnic campaigns in the former Yugoslavia, coupled with his rejection of Western values, were seen as one way of ensuring Slavic survival. The fact that Milosevic mobilized a form of Slavic socialism alongside his ultra-nationalism was also significant in Russia and its post-Soviet satellite states (Markotich 2000). For, as Slavism became significant within the nationalist revival, it also gathered momentum within forms of neo-communism. Significantly, the newly formed Communist Party of the Russian Federation (CPRF) drew much from Slavic patriotism and, as Zhirinovsky's appeal started to wane (or as he started to appear less and less consistent in his position), they began to take over the mantle of the major 'patriotic' opposition (Worth 2005: 131). Perhaps even more significant was the fact that the only oppositional communist parties to the CPRF were either more nationalist or more Stalinist in their orientation.

The renewal of Slavism as a national-populist response to the capitalist transition peaked in the 1990s. The emergence of Vladimir Putin as the Russian figurehead managed to dilute some of the more extreme responses that emerged at the end of the Soviet Union. Alternatively, Putin himself could be seen as the very instigator of such a Slavic movement, persuading states around him to look to Russia, as opposed to Brussels, for a form of statist inspiration. Certainly, since Putin took power in Moscow, Europe has been divided between those that aspire to join the European Union (EU) and those former Soviet states that still attach themselves to Mother Russia (Robinson 2012). On coming to office, Putin famously declared his vision of unifying the Russian traditions of 'statism', 'solidarity' and 'patriotism'. Yet, while Putin may have harboured a desire to become a leader in the traditional Slavic sense, the dissent that surrounds his leadership at the time of writing has a distinct nationalist and neo-communist flavour. In light of the questionable legality of the 2011 parliamentary elections and of his many political reforms, aimed at consolidating his position and his period of office as leader, the majority of dissenters originated not in Western or liberal forces (although they have also participated in the civil protests), but in the nationalist and communist forces that still make up a large section of the opposition within the Duma.[6] Therefore, while Putin has attempted to create a centrist and 'catch-all' position in order to marginalize potential Slavic extremism, this has ultimately remained problematic (Worth 2009).

Slavic populism in the post-Soviet states remains an interesting contradiction for outside observers. In light of the coloured revolutions in Georgia and the Ukraine and the embrace of Europe within the former Balkans and Baltic states, many have expressed a wish for Russia to follow suit. This has been even more noticeable in light of Putin's increasing centralization of power within Russia and as a result of several unexplained murders of high-profile critics of the government. Yet it is likely that any change to the Putin administration would unleash a new wave of Slavic extremism which might lead to fresh anti-Western and pro-nationalist movements that could become more dangerous for the stability of the global economy.

Islamophobia While, traditionally, far-right movements have centred upon Judaism and various socialist organizations as the main point of focus, Islamophobia, or, to borrow from the late Fred Halliday, 'Anti-Muslimism', has been the new focus (Halliday 1999). Its increase has been such that, in some cases, far-right organizations have made the peculiar switch from their anti-Semitic roots to backing the hard-line approach taken by the Israeli state against Palestine and Lebanon (Mayer 2004). The move towards this position was obviously accelerated after the attacks on the Twin Towers in New York, but the process had begun earlier, owing both to increased migration of Muslims to the West and the increase in fundamentalism in the Middle East from the Iranian revolution in 1979 onwards. Yet since 9/11, studies have indicated that the levels of racial or religious discrimination towards Muslim communities have dramatically increased (Sheridan 2006). In addition, according to some, the same forms of conspiracy that were being used by Hitler in *Mein Kampf* over International Jewry are being used to understand Islam. In other words, the belief that Muslims enter Western culture and manipulate it for their own gain is increasingly promulgated by some instigators of racial intolerance (Døving 2010).

The growth of 'Islamophobia' has also been reflected in popular literature, new organizations and certain notorious violent attacks. In the case of the former, anti-multicultural populist journalists such as Melanie Phillips have led attacks on the growing threat that Islamic fundamentalism has constituted in cities such as London. In the book *Londonistan*, Phillips argues that the liberal intelligentsia's pursuit of multiculturalism has allowed a subversive Islamic culture to grow and to spread instability within society (Phillips 2005). Other figureheads such as the former Dutch politician Pym Fortuyn also focused on the dangers of Islam. Like Phillips, Fortuyn portrayed himself as a self-confessed critic of multiculturalism from the liberal democratic tradition and, again like Phillips, he was an individual who previously had connections with politics of the left. Unlike Phillips, his entry into public life came through the field of politics as opposed to journalism. Fortuyn emerged in 2002 after declaring Islam to be a 'backward culture' and suggesting that Muslim immigration to the Netherlands should be immediately halted. Having been ostracized by all major parties, Fortuyn created his own Lijst Pim Fortuyn, named after himself, for the 2002 general election. During the campaign, Fortuyn was shot dead, but his party, which had been founded only months earlier, took 17 per cent of the popular vote, before slipping into obscurity within four years. Yet, despite its fall from grace, its sudden rise had shown that even in a country which had previously not experienced the growth of a far-right group, the breeding ground – as indeed indicated in studies just a few years earlier – was ripe for anti-Islamic extremism (Mudde and Van Holsteyn 2000). It is a position that has continued through the politics of Geert Wilders and his 'Party for Freedom'.

Both Phillips and Fortuyn could (and in the case of the former can) be seen as traditional intellectuals of the anti-Islamic right. Both claim to be rooted in the liberal tradition and see this tradition as being under threat from Islamic extremism that has been encouraged through the discourse of multiculturalism. Here, it is the multiculturalists who resemble the 'globalists' in their wider conspiratorial attempt to impose cultural relativism on civil society (Phillips 2005), while Muslims themselves and the ideology of Islam represent the actual wreckers. Such views have been reinforced by the emergence of new organizations that have been mobilized specifically to counter the threat of Islamism. Geert Wilders's group and groups such as the Swiss People's Party all have fear of Islamic immigration as the main focal point of their respective manifestos. Civil groups in Scandinavia, such as the twin-networked Stop Islamization of Norway (*Stopp islamiseringen av Norge*) and the Danish-originated Stop Islamization of Europe, have joined with organizations such as Robert Spencer's Stop Islamization of America or American Freedom in order to create wider international links. Spencer, like Phillips a best-selling writer of anti-Islamic books, has used social media to start blogs such as *Jihad Watch* and has been sponsored in his campaigns by the David Horowitz Freedom Center, which was set up to halt the move towards what was perceived as left-wing bias in academic teaching. Another group which has been endorsed by individuals such as Spencer has been the English Defence League. This has emerged through a number of demonstrations which, to quote Eatwell and Goodwin, link the 'football casuals movement' to street protests against Islam in significant multicultural centres. Their core targets have not necessarily been race, but the duel concepts of multi-faith and multi-ethnicity (Eatwell and Goodwin 2010: 7).

Islamophopia was to reach its extreme manifestation in July 2011 when a Norwegian cyber-activist, Anders Behring Breivik, shot a number of youth members of the Labour Party during an island work camp, while also bombing Oslo's government building, leaving over seventy-five people dead in total. The main focus of Breivik's attack was what he saw as an Islamic–Marxist plot aimed at overthrowing European civilization. He targeted the Norwegian Labour Party because of his conviction that it was they who had allowed this conspiracy to materialize. While this incident may have been an extreme and tragic extremist reaction to the idea of multiculturalism, it nevertheless drew from a body of reactionary and populist opinions that have all attempted to challenge mainstream perspectives. By drawing from conspiracy and mythology, right-wing radicalism has shown that it can alter the content of its narrative to explain changing threats to its own historical social development.

The trend towards anti-Islamic sentiment has, in some cases, altered the target of the far right's wrath. Yet, at the same time, it has largely been the issue of immigration and its control which has prompted the recent electoral success of the far right. Spurred by populist journalism, the main roots of discontent remain the management of immigration, which has led centrist political parties to move in to try to address such concerns. The main focus is not to construct a challenge to the form and content of global capitalism, but to respond to the consequences of what is perceived as globalism. It is the uneasy balance between the question of immigration management and that of a more radical reaction to globalization which has been noticeable in the recent resurgence of European far-right organizations.

The rise of the European far right

The problem of identifying a typology of what constitutes a far-right party or movement is one that has dogged comparative European political scientists since their re-emergence after the end of the Cold War (Ignazi 2003; Carter 2005; Hainsworth 2008). In general, they have included political organizations that have adopted core principles such as nationalism, xenophobia, populism and authoritarianism (Mudde 2007: 52). Unlike those who have studied globalization, neoliberalism and resistance in IPE and sociology at a macro level, few have understood the far right as a form of anti-globalization movement within the discourse of comparative European politics (Zaslove 2008). Few again have taken into consideration those far-right parties that have adopted an economic position that explicitly counters a market economy by favouring protectionism.

The first 'breakthrough' result for a new-style far-right party in western Europe is often considered to be Jorg Haider's success with the Austrian Freedom Party (Freiheitliche Partei Osterreichs, FPO), which broke through electorally in 1999, when it took 27 per cent of the vote. Populist, anti-multicultural and with a history of anti-Semitism, the party favoured the dramatic reduction of immigration and an Austrian-first policy in welfarism and business. Yet its attitude to neoliberalism has always been more complex. While it has argued for an Austrian-first approach to the economy, this has been promoted through support for small business as opposed to big corporations (Mudde 2007: 127), and is more indicative of an idealistic market society of the sort envisioned by Ron Paul than an expression of protectionism. Indeed, as a partner in the subsequent coalition government until 2005, the FPO did come under certain pressure from its own grass roots over its support for government neoliberal reforms. The subsequent split between Haider and the FPO (prior to his death in 2007) was one based not on ideological grounds, but on a clash of personalities – a trait that has continued to blight far-right organizations. Therefore, the subsequent organizations that have emerged from the FPO have continued to offer a similar economic outlook to that of their previous incarnation.

Following the success of the FPO, other organizations such as the Swiss People's Party (SVP) and Italy's regional Northern League (Lega Nord, LN) have pursued a greater commitment to market reform and to the reduction of state intervention in the economy. To a degree they have followed Thatcher's observation that it is precisely the 'left-wing humanitarian principles' that are pursued by social democratic parties and tolerated by Christian democratic parties which serve to actually limit the possibilities of neoliberal economic development (Thatcher 2002). Yet this position sits uneasily. It seems difficult from a far-right perspective to target some elements of cultural and social globalization, while appearing to condone its economic liberty. Some political groups have found that in order to distinguish themselves from mainstream politics, promoting a concrete alternative, the pursuit of protectionism, becomes attractive. As many comparative political studies are quick to note, far-right success in places such as Austria, Switzerland, the Netherlands and recently in Sweden has also been the result of a failure of the centre-right and centre-left to act as catch-all parties. In other words, to take up a position that extends beyond what is perceived as a narrow, pro-European, multicultural centrist consensus. Yet in places such as France and the UK, where Gaullists and conservatives have long since adopted a position that can co-opt potential extremes, the far right has explicitly looked at economic alternatives.

In France, the 2002 presidential campaign saw the seasoned nationalist campaigner Jean-Marie Le Pen beat Prime Minister Lionel Jospin for the opportunity to stand against Jacques Chirac for the final round. While this sent shock waves through France and the wider European community, Le Pen still managed to muster 20 per cent of the vote in the final contest. His party, the Front National (FN), had tapped into the growing anti-globalization feeling within France to move towards an anti-EU, anti-immigration, anti-neoliberal protectionist agenda. While it had previously been a proponent of free trade and the free market as a necessity against the excesses of communism, the FN changed tack in 1993, when, in light of the direction being taken at the Uruguay Round of GATT/WTO trade negotiations, it offered an alternative of French protectionism. This included supporting France's withdrawal from the EU and priority for the native French worker in the labour force. Yet Le Pen saw two other avenues that were open to him. First, he saw the reaction that mavericks such as Perot and Buchanan in the USA and also Pauline Hanson in Australia had attracted in their pursuit of a protectionist alternative.[7] Here, a firm set of positions within the developed world was being taken up to reject the policies of neoliberalism from a nationalist-protectionist perspective. For Le Pen, an opportunity arose for his party not just to make an economic U-turn but also to reach out to similar groups across the world to establish firm protectionist principles. As such, invitations to other far-right figures were extended at major FN rallies in order to facilitate dialogue between nationalists. Secondly, he saw that the general mood in France was such that globalist institutions were becoming more and more unpopular and figures such as the agriculturalist campaigner José Bové were becoming regarded as cult figures (Birchfield 2005). Therefore a coherent nationalist plan can exploit popular reactionary concerns over the World Bank, the IMF and the WTO, etc., by utilizing the French forms of exceptionalism.

If the FN have drawn success from their protectionist turn, then across the Channel the British National Party (BNP) have made significant ground in moving from an obsolete party connected with violence and direct attack to one which has managed to secure representation (Goodwin 2011). The far right first appeared in Britain through the National Front (NF). Favouring a confrontational anti-multicultural, extreme anti-immigration agenda, the NF peaked in the 1970s when they contested over three hundred seats and averaged 1.4 per cent of the vote in the 1979 general election, before quickly fading into a group that maintained links with football hooliganism and criminality. The rebirth of the far right as the BNP saw a similar trend, until the Cambridge-educated, highly articulate Nick Griffin became leader in 1999. Griffin turned the party into a British version of the French FN by moving away from an anti-Semitic stance to an Islamophobic one, by loosening its stance on the forced repatriation of ethnic minorities to one of voluntary repatriation, and promoting the idea of economic nationalism as one item of its central agenda. Griffin's own position on the free market was never more clearly stated than in the 2001 election manifesto, which underlined that:

> We are utterly opposed to globalisation and the idea that it's right
> for British workers to have to compete with cheap labour from

overseas ... When we set about rebuilding British industry behind tariff barriers, we have no intention of subsidising the same class of selfish traitors who lived off the sweat of ordinary workers for as long as possible, and then set about importing cheap non-white labour or exporting their capital and factories to the Far-East as soon as bad governments gave them the opportunity to do so. (BNP 2001)

Griffin's leadership has brought the party moderate success, in the form of the return of local councillors in specific areas and MEPs in the European elections.[8] Like the FN, it has also utilized the familiar conspiracy theories that, as this chapter has shown, have been central to the foundation of these movements' emergence. As early as 1992, Le Pen was claiming the EU to be part of a mythically conspired New World Order, while Griffin has understood the global economy to be one that allows for the forces of multiculturalism, Marxism, Islamism, Zionism and liberalism to develop around the pursuit of ruthlessness and the greed of elite individuals (Griffin 2002).

In Germany, the far-right response has been more extreme and less politically friendly. Yet at the same time they have been more explicit in their denunciation of neoliberal economics. The marginal success of the National Democratic Party (Nationaldemokratische Partei Deutschlands – Die Volksunion, NPD) in places such as Saxony, where it polled 9 and 5 per cent in the 2004 and 2009 elections respectively, has illustrated a significant re-emergence of nationalism within united Germany. Despite this, it has not replicated its success in the old West Germany, where its resurgence nearly took it past the 5 per cent threshold required for representation at the federal level. While not technically a neo-Nazi party, its flirtation with holocaust denial and with anti-Semitism has attracted such classification, as has its economic policy of favouring a national-social form of protection (Laqueur 1996). Its attack on neoliberalism and globalization has been the mainstay of its recent campaigns, with its call for an end to the neoliberal dominance of multinational corporations and of Anglo-American banks and the American cultural imperialism inherent within globalization (Steger 2005: 105–6). Yet in its inability to sever links with its past, it is largely 'International Jewry' and its manipulation of American finance which have formed the basis of its conspiratorial conception of the world. Unlike the FN and the

BNP, it has been keen to play up the 'fascist boot-boy image', by merging with more extreme parties such as the German People's Union (Deutsche Volksunion, DVU), as it did in 2011, and pledging support to Iran and the Palestinians in what they see as their unified struggle against Zionism.

Finally, from this we can try to broadly separate far-right groups into ones that reject the economic, cultural and social dimensions of globalism, from those that support the primacy of neoliberalism, but believe it should develop on their own terms. At the same time, there has also been another development in the rise of such attitudes. Groups have emerged that have shared some of the conspiratorial attributions of their far-right counterparts, yet have maintained their own commitment to liberal egalitarianism. Euro-sceptic groups such as the Danish People's Party and LN (which are often regarded as displaying strong far-right traits) and the United Kingdom Independence Party (UKIP) (which, despite sharing nearly all the policies and pretensions of the other two, has often evaded the charge) have combined to set up the Europe of Freedom and Democracy group in the European Parliament. Here, the EU and globalist developments such as climate change and international law are subjected to elitist claims that often border on the conspiratorial in their presentation. While the bloc is emerging as one that attempts to distinguish between economic and political forms of globalism, so distinguishing itself from the FN, the BNP and the NPD (it has also twice been in negotiations with the FPO, but as yet has not allowed them in), it does seem to adopt some of the populist conspiratorial myths that define far-right organizations. Therefore, while on one level such pro-neoliberal parties try to distance themselves from their racial, protectionist stance, they have also – increasingly – borrowed from the forms of populist rhetoric which the far right has used successfully.

Perhaps the one case whereby a far-right party has mobilized an explicit campaign across civil and political society can be seen with the recent rise of Golden Dawn movement (or *Avgi*) in Greece. Merging civil violence and protest with electoral success has seen the movement gain notoriety as the backlash to the economic crisis in Greece intensifies. Civil unrest has included office bombings, football hooliganism and the mobilization of a young front, while in the June election of 2012, Golden Dawn gained eighteen members in parliament. Nativist economic alternatives, anti-immigration and the conscious attempt to link the political with the civil has been a feature of the movement that can be understood as a way of forging a war of movement with a war of position within the instabilities of the situation in the country. Despite this, Golden Dawn (and Greece itself) does appear somewhat of a special case in this regard and it remains highly premature to assess the longevity of such a movement at this conjuncture.

Conclusion: a coherent alternative?

Based on the primacy of fear and informed by conspiracy theories, populist and nationalist reactions to globalism have been rife since the end of the Cold War and from the declaration by George Bush Snr that a 'New World Order' was emerging following the first Iraq war. Generally speaking the economic base for such a hegemonic alternative is a national protectionism that contests the moves towards the global neoliberal governance that emerged with the formation of the WTO and with the move towards the greater liberalization of the global economy. Individuals such as Ross Perot and Pat Buchanan in the USA and Pauline Hanson in Australia stressed the need for economic nationalism as an immediate response to the moves to liberalize trade and extend the power of foreign ownership of the economy. Yet the attack on economic neoliberal globalization has been overshadowed by the social and political costs of globalization. Immigration and multiculturalism remain the issues that fuel the conspiracies as these are the two social processes understood to have been imposed from 'above'. It is on these issues that conspiracy theories on the formation of an undemocratic liberal elite become attractive.

The hegemonic content of such a response has greater clarity in its economic base than progressive ones. It has a firm mercantilist direction that is based upon the isolationist principles of the past. However, when locating such a response, a number of shortcomings are evident. First, in articulating such a position, the departure point can become so absurd that it opens itself to ridicule. This is certainly the case with forms of conspiracy. If a conspiratorial ontology is to gain momentum as a social constructive reality, then it needs to distance itself from accusations of hatred and paranoia. The extreme nature of these provide an attraction that – even with the invention of new media formats – can often convince only those on the margins that such narratives are believable. Secondly, any movement based on the idea of conspiracy is rooted in racial and xenophobic forms of bigotry that are seen as backward and unacceptable in contemporary forms of liberal democracies. For any nationalist form of common sense to be able to realistically challenge the fabric of contemporary world order, it needs to be able to formulate its approach in such a way that such charges are neutralized. When looking at the public reaction to the growth of the far right in Europe, such moves are unlikely at present. Finally, the separation of the social attacks on immigration and multiculturalism that are inherent within nearly all populist criticisms of globalization, on the one hand, and the attack on economic globalization in the form of neoliberalism, on the other, have weakened the overall potential for a substantial, coherent transnational bloc of nationalist resistance. The fact that many organizations actually endorse the Thatcher–Reagan economic populism of the 1980s, while attacking multiculturalism, shows that there are many different sides to maintaining a far-right position in contemporary politics. Many of these do not attack (but on the contrary support) the economic fabric of neoliberalism. It also shows that Le Pen's vision of an international oppositional bloc of nationalist leaders that favour protectionist policies in order to challenge the hegemony of contemporary neoliberal common sense is a long way from being realized.

5 | THE RETURN OF GOD

> He was in the world, and the world was made by him, and
> the world knew him not (John 1:10)

The Iranian Revolution in 1979 proved to be a watershed in the future development of global politics as an uprising took place against a Western-backed regime that had been in power since the Second World War. The instability within Iran was not a secret, with the Shah's regime coming increasingly under stress since the MI5/CIA-funded coup against Mosaddegh's government in 1953. It was the long-standing fear that Iran would become an ally to the Soviets which provided the backing for the authoritarian regime of the Shah, and fear that any civil unrest would lead to a communist-backed takeover outweighed the possibility that it might lead to a functioning liberal democracy. By the mid-1970s it became impossible to contain civil unrest within the country, in light of the growing corruption and inequality of the Shah's regime. This led to debates in the Carter administration over whether the USA should support opponents of the regime in order to promote human rights and demand reforms to the existing system or support a crackdown on a civil opposition that might result in a Soviet-backed uprising (Seliktar 2000). What occurred instead seemed to take both superpowers by surprise, as the revolt that followed was one that was founded not upon political ideology but upon religious conservatism.

The knock-on effect of the uprising in Iran took time to grasp. The storming of the US embassy in Tehran and the subsequent weakening of US–Iran relations were seen as being unique in the modern history of the country, and not due to any long-term clash of ideologies. Here, the history between the USA and Iran, and the coup in 1953, led to assumptions that this was an isolated case, where a foreign power's past involvement made it a natural enemy to a new regime. This did not result in a change of US strategy towards similar Islamic movements. Indeed, the arming of the mujahedin in light of the Soviet invasion of Afghanistan proved to be a case in point. For, as recent accounts have mentioned, the belief in the longevity of West/East geopolitical containment was such that the consequences of what might have happened in the event of its conclusion were never considered (Thomas 2005). The Islamic system that the revolution instituted within Iran replaced the notion of politics through ideology with politics through the medium of God. For revolutionary Islamists, twentieth-century political ideologies were all part of the same Western product. All were imperialist forms of expression that had been transported to the developed world in the aftermath of decolonization. More importantly, all, in their own way, appeared ungodly in the manner in which they governed social and political relations. In the new Islamic Republic, the position of religion is centralized through the prominent position of clerics who interpret the word of God and facilitate this through common law and within everyday life.

For the spiritual leader and figurehead of the Iranian Revolution, the Ayatollah Khomeini (the 'Supreme Leader'), the revolution in Iran was intended to trigger similar revolutions across the world in pursuit of an Islamic global society. Despite originating in the minority Shia denomination, the Iranian Revolution saw a new form of hegemonic alternative emerge which would become increasingly appealing with the death of the socialist alternative at the end of the Cold War (Keddie 2003; Kepel 2006). At the same time, the revival of other forms of religion has also been a significant feature of politics which has challenged the secular appearance of the modern state. In the USA, for example, the rise of Christian fundamentalism, of born-again Christians, of creationism and of televangelism has led to the growth in significance of Christianity within political and civil society. Conservative forms of Hinduism, commonly found within Indian nationalism and within political movements and organizations in India, and Haredi Judaism, found in similar organizations in Israel and in the USA, have all increased in significance since the free market claimed victory over socialism. Arguments have also been made that places such as Sri Lanka have been marred in their historical development by ongoing forms of Buddhist fundamentalism (Bartholomeusz and De Silva 1998). Yet, while there has been a significant increase in both the amount of fundamentalist religious practice and in its significance in world politics, the idea that it should form the basis of a hegemonic challenge to neoliberalism remains more complex. Unlike economic global reform or protectionism, hegemonic projects that place religion at their heart can complement existing orders or can provide the main platform for an economic system to emerge to contest an existing order.

Religion as a hegemonic agent

As noted in earlier chapters, Gramsci's own writings on religion were both numerous and extensive. His study of the Catholic Church and its role in facilitating consent within Italy made up a significant part of his writing.[1] Of particular importance was the role of intellectuals within the Church and the distinctions between the traditional roles of the clergy and the role that the Church had in popular culture (Gramsci 1971: 14–23; Gramsci 1992: 162–3; Gramsci 1995: 1–137). This interest extended to other faiths, denominations and religions, and he was particularly interested in the development of what he termed the Protestant pan-Christian movement and its activities at the international level (Gramsci 1996: 386). What is of interest in Gramsci's understanding of religion is that it appears as a form of agency that should largely be engaged with, as opposed to one that should somehow be eradicated. Here Gramsci is highly dismissive of contemporary Marxist understandings of religion; the most profound Soviet political theorist at the time, Nikolai Bukharin, was quite forthright and dismissive in his views on religion. Religion would and must be transcended, when the proletariat realized that its main purpose was as a tool of class oppression (Bukharin 1925). Gramsci argued that this misunderstood the dynamic of religion and how it is used and understood at different levels of society. As religion (or, for Gramsci, Catholicism) is interpreted in different ways and understood differently by different sections of society, then it has no single meaning or purpose within society (Gramsci 1971: 419–25). The common sense that is driven from religion produces different results and different understandings of the way the world works and functions (or contrasting conceptions of the world; Murray and Worth 2012). Therefore, religion can be seen as a sort of a neutral agent. It can be utilized as part of a progressive or reactionary counter-hegemonic project or it can be used in order to facilitate an existing one. Alternatively, as this chapter will argue, it can be used to form the basis of an economic and social system that provides a separate challenge to the prevailing order.

In the first case religion can play a significant role in successfully mobilizing a war of position. Gramsci himself looked at religious movements that were often tied to the state so that they could be mobilized together as part of a wide socialist programme (Gramsci 1995). In contemporary terms, the leftist theology and campaigns utilized by parts of the Catholic, Methodist and Anglican churches can be seen as a component of the internationalist progressive left that was outlined in Chapter 3. The emergence of liberation theology in Latin America and the Christian element that was implicit within the guild socialist movement provide us with examples of such cases. In Islam, Ibn Khaldun's philosophies of social cohesion add to the potential for a transformative process, and the additional democratic uprisings of the Arab Spring that were prominent through 2011 provide another practical impetus for progressive change. For the subaltern classes, romantic mythology and folklore also played a large part in the construction of common sense and are used as ways of successfully organizing religion. For example, the role of organic intellectuals in facilitating religious study groups and in communicating the stories and narratives of religious figures has long been a key component in the growth of specific religious belief (ibid.: 188–91; Billings 1990; Murray and Worth 2012). For this to be deployed within a progressive context, religions of all types need to focus upon the function such religious figures played in reducing inequality and promoting social solidarity.

The recent work of Kyle Murray has showed us that popular religion can play a role in promoting the idea of free markets and neoliberalism. His work on the prosperity gospel and on the rise of evangelical Pentecostalism has shown how Christianity can appear as a central agent for the development of entrepreneurial common sense. The spread of televangelists and of mass forms of new media and communications networks has created a new arena in which Christianity can expand. What is more striking about this development is that it appears as an organic transnational movement (Murray 2012). While many evangelical groups have emerged from and been associated with the USA, their emergence has been more prominent in the developing world. Sub-Saharan Africa has in particular seen a rise in Pentecostal Christianity, with the prosperity gospel playing a significant role in its growth. In promoting the free market and business initiatives through the medium of God, faith-based organizations and associations have been set up that provide education for future business leaders (Murray and Worth 2012). In this instance, religion is used to develop neoliberal capitalist consciousness and common sense. The successful building of organic religious groups alongside free market ideology has allowed for new relationships within the developing world that have all enhanced the consolidation of neoliberal hegemony.

The relationship between capitalism and the 'Protestant ethic' is a long-standing one that was rooted within the socio-economic development of Europe and was to become synonymous with the Weberian understandings of sociology. Yet the building of capitalism alongside Christianity in the developing world was a product of colonialism that re-emerged during the Cold War, when the Soviet alternative was characterized as 'ungodly'. As Augelli and Murphy outline, the USA looked to the strength of the Christian faith in Africa to stave off the threat of communism and to foster capitalist development. This was aided through US-based religious organizations that invested in and made close links with the grassroots development of the Church, especially in the aftermath of independence as a result of post-colonialism (Augelli and Murphy 1988). The same could be said of other religions at the time. The British Empire, for example, was renowned for its commitment to the retention of existing traditions and beliefs within their dominions. This devolved hierarchal system of governance that spread from Malaya and India through to parts of Arabia was designed to mould religious differences and traditions in order that they would be compatible with wider British economic interests. During the Cold War, the USA adopted an approach which looked to gain the support of leaders in the Islamic world in return for aid and strategic support against potential Soviet aggression. Thus, arch-authoritarian states such as Saudi Arabia were given free rein and support to develop a hard-line Islamic regime in return for a prominent anti-Soviet stance.

Yet the support that the USA gave to such regimes allowed a series of social forces to emerge to form an alternative challenge to what became the post-Cold War reality. Religion here has played an oppositional role in a number of ways. First, it has attracted opposition to social change by contesting the fabric of consumerism that has emerged with the era of globalization. To a degree, religious contestation holds some similarities with the reactionary and nationalist forms that were discussed in the last chapter. Conservative reactions to social liberalization and to the so-called loosening of traditional morals are evident through both avenues of critique. However, in the case of religion, it is through the interpretation of religious texts rather than nationalism that answers are provided to these concerns (Kepel 1994). Modern capitalism thus displays excesses that endanger the way common life should be ordered as defined by the scriptures. Again this does not necessarily have to be understood as an attack on the overall nature of global capitalism. Moves to protect society from the excesses of the market were an integral part of Polanyi's account of nineteenth-century liberal capitalism (see Chapter 2) and in many cases were due to a fear of negative consequences that might occur if it was not controlled. To an extent, the religious revival in global politics can be seen as responding to what are perceived as the potential negative or 'ungodly' effects of the global market (Munck 2007). From the debate in the Islamic world over the implementation and upholding of sharia law through to the condemnations of sexual freedoms that have been common among Christian fundamentalist organizations in North America, religion has acted as a way of contesting the immorality that market consumerism might bring.

For a counter-hegemony project to take shape, a clear economic alternative rooted in religious principles needs to be imagined. Sharia law goes some way to prompting such a development as it states that God takes preference over private ownership. As a result there is a commitment to share God's wealth evenly across society, and some radical interpretations of this can contest corporate power and unregulated private enterprise on religious grounds. This offers an economic alternative that provides an attractive notion for subaltern classes in the developing world. It is often said that one of the main attractions of Marxism-Leninism to the developing world was that it offered an alternative route to development to capitalist industrialization (Lane 1996). The proviso of equality and social solidarity appeared appealing to newly formed states that had struggled against Western capitalism during the fight for independence. Likewise, religious alternatives have appealed to civil society in the developing world that has felt alienated or ostracized by globalization (Haynes 2007). The idea of traditional social responsibilities coupled with an economic agenda that appears more moral in the eyes of God is similarly attractive in the era of neoliberalism. Despite this, it appears that Islamic political economy is more advanced in advocating an alternative economic project to neoliberalism than the fundamentalism provided by Christianity and other religions such as Hinduism. There have been opportunities and potential avenues for such non-Islamic religions to create such frameworks, but as yet these have not been developed as coherently.

Global political Islam

Islamic responses to neoliberalism have attracted a recent flurry of analytical accounts of their significance within global politics (Barber 1996; Butko 2004; Mandaville 2007; Evans 2011). Benjamin Barber's *Jihad vs McWorld* provided an interesting antidote to Huntington in the aftermath of 9/11. While he argues that a confrontation between Western and Islamic forces has emerged, he also stresses that this has been exacerbated not just by excess but also by fear (Barber 1996, 2004). The centre-left tone of his arguments, which are underlined by his belief in dialogue to facilitate understanding of the Islamic world, provides a riposte to the doomsday scenarios that the American right were putting forward at the time. Yet, while Barber does point to the fallacies of neoliberalism in contributing to the rise of religious extremism, he points out that it also has the tendency to treat Islam as 'a monolithic Islam, opposed in every respect to the values that describe some equally monolithic version of the "west"' (quoted in Evans 2011: 1751).

If we look at Islam's potential as a counter-hegemonic project, then work by Butko and Evans offers two examples where such a case is made. Here, Islam is seen as a political project that espouses a coherent revolutionary ideological conception alongside a clear functional strategy of realizing this through the construction of a state (Butko 2004: 49–51). Evans takes this farther and suggests that political Islam can be seen as a counter-hegemonic challenge to neoliberalism in four different ways. The first of these, he argues, is through the rejection of the Enlightenment tradition and the idea of 'truth through reason' and its replacement with 'truth through revelation' (Evans 2011: 1758–60). The second is economic and concerns the principles of private property that are covered by sharia law, while the third relates to the preferment of the premise of 'duties and community' over the premise of universal human rights (ibid.: 1758–66). Finally, as the revolutionary development of Iran post-1979 shows, the Islamic state is one that centralizes its governmental structure so it is accountable not to popular representation but to God (ibid.:

1768–9). Following on from these analyses we can now assess some of the developments that have occurred in the Islamic world to see whether they stand up as vibrant challengers to neoliberal capitalism.

The Islamic state The revolution in Iran brought with it a revival of an Islamic opposition to the secular state that sought to return God to the forefront of politics. Yet, despite the emergence of political Islam, the Islamic republics and monarchies that were in existence prior to 1979 have had mixed experiences in the way that radicalism has been managed. In the case of Pakistan and Saudi Arabia, radical Islam has been managed amid a growing radicalization of civil society. Both the Islamic Republic of Pakistan and the Kingdom of Saudi Arabia have relied upon strong leadership in order to soak up potential radicalism. In Pakistan, Islamic fundamentalism sat uneasily alongside secularism, liberal democracy and militarism. When instabilities have threatened the overall stability of the political and civil society of the country, military coups have occurred. At the height of the Cold War, Pakistan's military dictatorship created strong ties with the USA, but it was the coup led by Zia ul-Haq which sought to engage with Islamic traditions by establishing a sharia legal code, a banking tax in line with the Islamic tradition of redistribution and a higher concentration of Islamic education. Part of this was an attempt to contain religious social forces in the country, which, in light of the events occurring in Iran, threatened to bubble over (Mandaville 2007: 174). The Musharraf coup in 1999 was again a response to internal instabilities but in this case the decision was taken to forge certain alliances with Islamic forces to form a coalition in government. In Saudi Arabia, the potential religious backlash and the favourable relationship with the USA have been tempered by the maintenance of an ultra-conservative society. Attempts at containing the Wahhabi or Salafi traditions within the country[2] have been more difficult given the increase in transnational forms of radicalism. The fact that many of the terrorist activities of such groups featured a high number of individuals who originated from Saudi Arabia has placed strains on both the internal dynamics of the country and its relationship with the West.

In both cases, the use of a strong authoritarian leadership in order to smooth over potential instabilities is one that Gramsci refers to as the process of 'Caesarism'. This is where there is a lack of consensus between competing social forces that is relieved only when a strong leader steps in to take charge and initiate political change (Gramsci 1971: 219–20). However, while this appears as a useful temporary measure to stem such instabilities and ideological clashes within political society, it becomes very difficult to sustain over time unless a solid hegemonic civil society is built to support it. One could argue that under ul-Haq and under the structure of the royal family in Pakistan and Saudi Arabia respectively, this was being achieved, but the recent resurgence of Islamic radicalism has made instability more difficult to contain. The same might be said of Malaysia. As John Hilley's excellent account of Malaysia shows, its long-serving leadership under Mahathir Mohamad attempted to co-opt Islam alongside industrial development and later through market economics. This brought with it a rise in a more conservative Islamist opposition (politically represented by the Pan Malaysian Islamic Party, or PAS) that has made an impact in post-Mahathir Malaysia (Hilley 2001: 178–89). Yet the threat that such an opposition might pose to Malaysia's homogeneous system has been diluted through the political process of coalition-building with other ideological groups and traditions.

The fragilities in Pakistan and growing fragilities in Saudi Arabia, alongside the potential for radicalism in places such as Malaysia, have been overshadowed by the growth of Islamic radicalism in what are often defined as 'failed states'. The success of groups such as Hamas and Hezbollah in Palestine and Lebanon respectively has shown how radical political Islam can be utilized within nationalist movements in civil disputes. Radical Islamic factions have been seen to have played a role in the unrest that has blighted many unstable states. Yemen, Sudan and Somalia, for example, have experienced severe unrest involving extreme Islamic factions each seeking to establish anti-Western regimes. The most notorious here was in Afghanistan under the Taliban, which lasted in government from 1996 to 2011. After the fall of the Communist Party from power in 1992, the mujahedin fragmented into rival competing camps that would see the country slip into civil war. The Taliban was one such group that emerged from the rubble of a conflict that saw many neighbouring states fund and supply different fighting factions (Saikal 2004). Upon taking power, the Taliban sought to build an ultra-fundamentalist system of Islamic rule, whereby sharia law was interpreted in its most austere form and the economy became reliant upon contributions from international traffickers (Mandaville 2007: 228). Rather than create a social and political system that could rival neoliberalism in the West, it created one that became so draconian and removed from socio-economic global developments that it simply became unsustainable. The aftermath of the acts of September 11th would finish off the fragile regime as the USA attacked in retaliation for its noted links with Bin Laden and al-Qaeda.

If others had failed to follow the lead taken by Iran, what of the Iranian state itself? The global neoliberal revolution proved to be hard for the state to resist on its own idealist terms, and by the mid-1980s it looked towards market economic reform. After the death of Khomeini at the end of the decade, this process speeded up and saw a struggle in the 1990s between reformists, conservatives and hard-liners. The landslide election victory for the reformist Mohammad Khatami in 1997 brought in a fresh set of social forces that favoured greater openness and a reinterpretation of the nature and objectives of the revolution. This would include ongoing debate at the political and the clerical level of the state. Further advances in this direction were seen with the landslide victory of the Reformist Coalition at the 2000 parliamentary elections, and with Khatami's re-election in 2001, where he won nearly 80 per cent of the vote. Yet it was here that the reform movement started to face a backlash from the clerics and conservatives, fearful that the state was moving against the wishes of God and its revolutionary purpose (Keddie 2003). The fear that such reforms would lead to a move towards secularization was not helped by George W. Bush's declaration during his State of the Union address in 2002 that in its present form Iran was a rogue state and formed part of an 'axis of evil'. At least symbolically this drove home the message to the religious hierarchy in Iran that the threat from the liberal West was as great as before and the reform movement needed to be quelled. Subsequently, the Council of Guardians, the prestigious constitutional committee appointed by the Supreme Leader[3] that subjected electoral procedure to religious and legal scrutiny, banned a large proportion of reformists from standing at the 2004 parliamentary elections. This led to an ideological shift back to a religious/conservative-dominated legislature and the election of the populist Ahmadinejad in 2005 (Adib-Moghaddam 2007).

Since 2005, Ahmadinejad has assumed a similar Caesarist position to leaders in Saudi Arabia and Pakistan, with the distinct difference that he is trying to maintain the revolutionary spirit as opposed to containing it. Increasingly aided by the Revolutionary Guards, Ahmadinejad has taken a nationalist, anti-Western stance in foreign affairs. In a move reminiscent of populist positions taken by Western far-right parties that were discussed in the previous chapter, Ahmadinejad has openly attacked the state of Israel and, while addressing the UN, has argued that the attacks on September 11th were the result of an 'inside US conspiracy'. He has also played the 'anti-imperialist' card by courting the populist authoritarian left, forging 'revolutionary bonds' with leaders such as Chávez in Venezuela and Ortega in Nicaragua. With the demonstrations that followed his re-election in 2009 and a boycott of the 2012 parliamentary elections by members of the Green movement (reform movement), it remains to be seen how long the authoritarian stance can be maintained. This is especially true in light of the Arab Spring movements in North Africa that brought civil contestation right to the forefront of societies across the Arabic and Islamic world.

Transnational radical Islam Transnational radicalism among Islamists is geared towards the attempt to unify an Islamic civilization against statist and nationalist divides that have stemmed the potential for an alternative hegemonic project to be envisaged at a truly global level. As Barber pointed out in his metaphorical account of the emergence of neoliberal and religious fundamentalists, one does not stand as the total opposite to the other as they both see the world as a global entity and not one separated by borders. They also use and are reliant upon forms of communication and technological advances to mobilize their cause. The world of the 'Jihad' thus emerges via the world of 'McWorld' (Barber 1996: 156–7). For transnational radicals or Islamic globalists, resistance to the neoliberal world is drawn from a commitment to contest society at every level. The methods of such contestation include non-violent methods of radicalism, organized through study groups and networks led by organic intellectuals with the objective of gaining ideological support for a global Islamic polity. They also include forms of Salafi jihadism that maintain that there is an Islamic duty of self-sacrifice and violent struggle that will be rewarded in the afterlife. To a certain extent the former represents a war of position, in the sense that it is geared towards ideological confrontation; while the latter can be seen as a form of war of movement, despite the fact that the act resulting from jihad might be counterproductive in reality.

Historically, the idea of contemporary pan-Islamism can be traced to the growth of the Muslim Brotherhood in Egypt from the 1920s onwards. The Brotherhood, whose slogans included the phrase 'death for the sake of Allah is our goal', has as its initial objective the revival of Islam so that the Koran gains centrality in the ordering of society, politics and the economy. The Brotherhood has altered its strategy and intent throughout its history, but has striven to forge establishments across the Islamic world in order to coordinate specific goals and mobilization. Its spread to Yemen, Jordan, Syria and Palestine by the 1930s, and then after the Second World War across to neighbouring North African states, has enabled it to gain significance in Sunni Islamic societies at a time when ideological secularism was dominant and both superpowers looked to gain influence in the region. It also has organizations in Muslim communities in the West. It has been accused many times by states and regimes of subversive tactics, and its recent activities were associated with the civil demonstrations against Mubarak in Egypt during the Arab Spring, where its involvement led to a mobilization against similar regimes in other Arabic states. While the Brotherhood itself has pledged to reinvent itself as a civil movement for democratization (Helbawy 2010), it still attracts criticism as a destabilizing force in the region which is ultimately opposed to secularization.[4]

The Muslim Brotherhood provided a platform of transnational networks and enabled the birth of pan-Islamic civil society. It also allowed the spirit of Islamic radicalism to continue during the era of power politics. The emergence of radicalism in this aftermath owes more to its transnational vision than to its ideological development. Groups associated with transnational radicalism in the post-Cold War era tend to have become associated with Salafism, often regarded as adopting the most historically literal interpretation of Islam. Peter Mandaville identifies three trends of transnational Salafist radicalism: the 'quietists', the 'Islamists' and the 'Jihadis' (Mandaville 2007: 248–9). The 'quietists' are those who believe Islamic transformation will emerge from individual religious enlightenment, while 'Islamists' believe that there is an active duty to convert society at large. Both these favour a radical form of Islamic alternative to contemporary capitalism, but believe that this should come about through ideological contestation at the level of civil society – a classical representation of the war of position. The 'Jihadis' take a view that it is the duty of Muslims to undertake an active mission in order to achieve such a transformation. For the Jihadis, this is a requirement that is explicit within the Koran and one that is essential for revolutionary Islamic change. Yet as a form of war of movement it has been less convincing. While violent episodes such as the Madrid, London and Bali bombings and the events of 9/11 have had a significant impact on the nature of global politics, their expression as a form of hegemonic contestation has been less coherent. Salafism has led to forms of political Islam that reject the contemporary state system and believe in a global system, but the method of jihad as a practical tool does not seem to suggest specific indications of what a global Islamic order would look like. Recent studies on Salafist jihadism have suggested that the prominence of al-Qaeda has allowed previously disperse groups committed to Islam to unite around a single theme (Turner 2012). Groups working under the al-Qaeda umbrella have thus emerged across wide areas of Africa, Central Asia and the Middle East, being especially active in conflict zones. Here the strategy at least appears to be based upon a 'think global, act local' basis, as although jihad is practised against the 'ungodly' enemy in areas where the jihadist lives, it is being undertaken for a global cause (ibid.).

In terms of the battle within civil society, the war of position has been waged by groups such as Hizb ut-Tahrir, organic intellectuals such as Abu Hamza al-Masri, Omar Bakri Muhammad and Anjem Choudary, who have all been based (or in the case of the former imprisoned) at some time in the UK, as well as more formal, less aggressive traditional intellectuals such as Ata Abu Rashta and Ismail Yusanto and the works of Taqiuddin al-Nabhani. They argue that a centralized global Islamic state, often referred to as a caliphate, is a goal that all Muslims should strive for. The pan-Islamic organization Hizb ut-Tahrir believes that this can be achieved by non-violent means through conversion and the power of ideas. The methods that are employed for this to be achieved, however, have left it open to criticism. For example, through its preaching and its literature it has been accused of inciting racial and religious hatred. It has been banned in many parts of the Arabic world and in Russia under terrorist laws over its support of Muslims in Chechnya. It has also been banned in Germany for anti-Semitic racism and has been condemned by many think tanks and policy bureaus in the USA. The aggressive stance taken towards Jewish and Western practices is apparent through populist condemnations by speakers and figureheads that have resulted in confrontations with opposing groups in multicultural societies (Githens-Mazer 2010). It can also be seen in the influential work of al-Nabhani himself, in which he condemns Western and secular forms of Islam as ones that have largely emerged through a collection of colonial and neo-imperialist conspiracies (al-Nabhani 1995). Like the Muslim Brotherhood, however, it has also argued that it has been discriminated against by authoritarian regimes and, as a civil organization, appears as a potentially democratizing force against such governments. In Uzbekistan, for example, it has won support from human rights NGOs and campaigners in their struggle against authoritarianism.

What are we to make of such transnational groups when looking at hegemonic contestation? Unlike those that seek to build an Islamic state, they appear to be in favour of an alternative that transcends the state system and explicitly reject any attempts to be somehow subsumed back into it as other revolutionary doctrines have long been. The establishment of a global caliphate is the overall objective of radical transnational Islam. The methods by which this would be achieved remain highly untenable. The notion of jihadism has become so synonymous with al-Qaeda and terrorism that it remains at the extremes of common acceptability, and while Islamic Salafists do have a coherent political and economic programme that is distinctly counter-hegemonic and can be seen in the writings of al-Nabhani (1995, 1996), they remain highly marginalized within the wider Islamic world.

Other fundamentalist responses

Looking at the manner in which other religions have reacted to the forces of globalization, none has had the same impact on global politics as political Islam, but some have still made a significant revival in recent years. Fundamentalist forms of Christianity have seen a rise in popularity on a global scale, with their social responses to what they perceive as the immoral practices of an increasingly permissive society. Both Christianity and the revival of Hinduism in India are often understood as forms of conservative reactions to transformation. Yet, like political Islam, they should not merely be understood in the same vein as the traditional reactionary movements that were covered in the previous chapters. Both, in their own way, contain revolutionary elements – whether in the form of self-enlightenment from being 'born again' or from a conviction that religious belief repels previous imperialist forces. They have also flourished among lower-income groups in developed countries and have made the greatest 'conversions' in developing societies (Jenkins 2002).

Christian fundamentalism The departure point for the study of Christian fundamentalism is often seen as being within the USA (Augelli and Murphy 1988; Marsden 2008), yet its roots go back far beyond this to the Reformation and the birth of Puritanism and the subsequent colonial development in North America. As mentioned above, contemporary accounts have argued that many of the new forms have arisen in the developing world owing to evangelical preachers native to that area, and they have indeed had an impact on central Christian markets such as the USA (Murray 2012). However, when looking at the roots of Christian fundamentalism, the impact made by individuals such as Jerry Falwell, Pat Robertson and Ralph Reed and by organizations such as the Christian Coalition cannot be ignored. The Christian Coalition is a significant pressure group that has wielded great influence on (largely Republican) politicians and specific administrations and is committed to a belief that Christianity needs 'to play an active role in government again like never before' in order to maintain the 'hard work of freedom' (Christian Coalition 2012). Politically, the Coalition has advocated opposition to public health reforms on the basis that taxpayers would have to pay for abortions, opposition to the appointment of 'liberal' constitutional judges, the banning of homosexuals from army service and opposition to the funding of human embryonic stem cell research. In addition, it is also supportive of a reduction in taxation, which it believes is essential to personal liberty and freedom.

On first viewing, the positions taken up by the Christian Coalition seem to reinforce conservative readings of neoliberalism. Its debt to Ronald Reagan and to Reaganomics is mentioned in much of its literature, and the links to the Republican Party are notorious, but despite this the Coalition can also inspire ideas that appear to contest the fabric of the contemporary neoliberal order. For example, its leader and founder, Pat Robertson, was highly influential among conspiracy theorists with his book *The New World Order*, written in 1991 (see the last chapter). Here a religious interpretation is added to the conviction that an elitist plot is being constructed. Citing various biblical sources, such as the struggle for good and evil during Armageddon that is often referred to in Revelation, Robertson suggests that such elites are formed upon a godless ideology that is geared towards creating 'a new world order for the human race under the domination of Lucifer and his followers' (Robertson 1991: 37; also quoted in Rupert 2000: 111). The crossover with the Patriot Movement is also evident, with arguments from evangelicals and Christian organizations that international organizations are ungodly regimes. For example, in its campaign for the USA to leave the United Nations the John Birch Society observes: 'Unlike the US, the UN does not recognise the supremacy of God and views itself as the source of rights. As the source, it can give and take away "rights" at its whim. In addition any government body strong enough to govern the world would be strong enough to oppose the world' (John Birch Society 2000).

Here, God is centralized above forms of political agency, adopting a position similar to that of Allah within Islamic states. Some studies have also shown how such religious movements are twinned with wider nationalist projects. Mark Rupert's studies on the far right in the USA, for example, portray forms of Christian fundamentalism within a wider family of American protectionist exceptionalism, with the Christian Coalition borrowing from organizations such as the John Birch Society and Liberty Lobby and vice versa (Rupert 2000: 110–12). However, the global spread of Pentecostalism appears to be a movement that moves well beyond campaigns mobilized at the national level.

There have been significant rises in evangelical Christianity in Africa, South Korea and Brazil, which have made challenges to the manner in the way global culture is increasingly consumed (Lechner and Boli 2005: 174). Some have argued that this has indeed formed an oppositional position to the processes of globalization, which are seen as secular and immoral in nature (Castells 1997: 25). As the evangelical movement is geared towards the idea of the second coming, it is very supportive of the state of Israel. A central message of the movement is that as Israel and the 'Holy Land' provide the geographical location for such a coming, a Jewish settlement should be in place when it occurs. The origins of this conviction can be traced back to the birth of Puritanism in the seventeenth century, but is perhaps most associated with the birth of Christian Zionism, which resurfaced two centuries later in certain Protestant circles. Biblical interpretations of the second coming and Armageddon mention that the name 'Armageddon' stems from a field north of Jerusalem where the battle is to be staged, and that the regions should be settled by the 'descendant of Abraham' at the time (Wagner 1998). Support for the maintenance of the Israeli state has not just been a feature of American evangelicals who have gained celebrity status – such as Jerry Falwell – but has also been the central message of evangelical Pentecostals across the world (Murray 2012).

The support for Zionism as a core part of the global evangelical movement demonstrates a distinct difference to the anti-Semitism often associated with the far right. This can be seen with Robertson's reading of the New World Order. For him, the global elite was not founded by a Masonic-Judaist elite per se but by those aligned to a global Satanist plot (Robertson 1991: 70–2). Yet Robertson does find some common ground with the Islamophobia that is inherent within the new extreme right that I outlined in the last chapter. Such is Robertson's commitment to the Jewish cause in Israel that he has suggested that Ariel Sharon's stroke, which left him incapacitated in 2006, was the divine result of him having given up land to the Palestinians. Mavericks such as Robertson might provide an extreme representation of such Zionist sentiments, but its message is relayed across media networks such as the GOD Channel, an international evangelical television broadcaster whose global characteristics are reflected by the fact that it was formed by South Africans working in London and broadcasts from Jerusalem.

Christian fundamentalism has made a significant impression in terms of its strength[5] and impact as a pressure group on social matters at a global level. It also forms the basis of a counter-hegemonic ideology, especially when viewed through the lens of Huntington's clash of civilizations thesis and the forthcoming holy clash with Islamism. In terms of mounting a sustained challenge to neoliberalism as a whole, it is less significant. Much of what the evangelical movement contributes is tied to the wider principles of the free market, albeit through the medium of Christian values. The promotion of the prosperity gospel by the GOD Channel and other leading organic intellectuals has led to the link between Christianity and entrepreneurial capitalism.

While its emergence might contest or try to reorient some aspects of globalization which appear to have an ungodly and unchristian character, and some of its rhetoric has the potential to strengthen a reactionary counter-hegemonic bloc, its own appearance is not necessarily oppositional.

Hinduism While the very nature of fundamentalist Hinduism might appear contradictory, Hindu political and civil organizations in India and Nepal have sought to contest multiculturalism in South Asia. Violent clashes between Hinduist groups and Christians, Sikhs and Muslims have marked the post-colonial history of India, with specific events in Gujarat, Mumbai (or Bombay as it was then) and Kashmir seeing great religious tension. Its emergence as a political force has become more evident since the end of the Cold War and through India's engagement with the global economy. Hindu nationalism or Hindutva is often managed and correlated through the umbrella group Sangh Parivar, which emerged in the 1960s to represent Hindu-inspired civil and political groups. Some of the organizations that feature in the group, such as the Rashtriya Swayamsevak Sangh, have existed since the anti-colonial movement and aim to uphold the cultural and social traditions of Hinduism, while others, such as the Bharatiya Janata Party (BJP) and Shiv Sena are political parties that have representation in the national parliament. In this way, Sangh Parivar provides a vehicle for political and civil society groups whereby hegemonic strategies can be formed (Berglund 2011).

In what ways, then, have such organizations contested, or shown the potential to contest, neoliberal globalization? The remit of Hindu nationalism is to revise the colonial effect that the British had on Indian culture and life and to restore it to its former mono-religious state. Clashes with opposing religions are commonplace as religions such as Christianity and Islamism are viewed as being 'foreign' and imported in its colonial past (Anderson 1991). Likewise, globalization has been denounced as a new form of Western imperialism, geared towards attacking traditional Indian culture and posing a new threat to the future of Hinduism. As argued by one such supporter and writer:

> [The] Macaulayism of British India has become in letter and spirit the Globalization of today. Pound Sterling has been replaced by the US Dollar. To the people of India in general and educated

Indians in particular, Globalisation seems to be rather mild and well meaning, more like an imperceptible breeze, which blows in silently, fills up the psychological atmosphere, creates a mental mood, inspires an intellectual attitude and finally settles down as a cultural climate, pervasive, protean and ubiquitous. It is not out to use a specified section of Indian society as a vehicle of its virulence. It is not like Islamism which wants to destroy the body of a culture in one fell sweep. It is not subtle like Christianity which subverts a society surreptitiously. Yet at the same time, it is a creeping tox-aemia which corrodes the soul of our Hindu culture and corrupts our time-honoured social systems in slow stages. And its target is every section of Indian society. (Sundaram 2006)

Yet despite these assertions, the political representatives of Hindutva themselves do not necessarily appear to oppose free market capitalism. The BJP supports free market capitalism and small government and was a key player in the centre-right National Democratic Alliance, which was in power from 1998 to 2004 and did much to encourage the economic boom that has marked India's recent engagement with the global economy. Similarly, others believe that the manner in which globalization is understood in India is highly compatible with Hindu nationalism. For example, Meera Nanda argues that the success brought about by India's experience with globalization has instilled a jingoistic defence of Hindu nationalism. As Islamic neighbours have failed in terms of their recent economic development, the Indian economic system has prospered, which shows the superiority of its political and cultural system (Nanda 2010). Rather than promoting secularization, India, continues Nanda, promotes the 'de-secularisation of society' that has resulted in 'new technologies and institutional arrangements providing new opportunities for traditional religions to modernise themselves and penetrate deeper into the pores of the society' (ibid.: 4).

Like radical Islamism and evangelical Christianity, fundamentalist Hinduism has been employed in a number of ways and has been enhanced by the revolutions made in media technology. It can be used both as a form of contestation of neoliberalism and alternatively as an agent for hegemonic consolidation. What is unique is that owing to the economic success that India has had in attracting investment, it has embodied this religion within a wider nationalism that encourages a superiority complex regarding its Islamic neighbours. The tensions that this might cause within India provide another interesting dynamic to the overall stability of the global economy. As with Pentecostal Christianity's support of Zionism, the mobilization of extreme forms of Hindu nationalism might spark off renewed religious clashes in the region. In addition, the balance between Hindutva as a hegemonic tool and Hindutva as a form of contestation may swing significantly as a result of future events. The BJP might at present favour free market reform, but it could alter its perception and revert to understanding globalism as a foreign threat. In the aftermath of successive election defeats and amid claims that it is on the decline (Hannon 2010), it might reassess its support for free market economics in a manner similar to that of nationalist organizations in Europe. This populist route might be employed as a new method of re-establishing itself as a political force.

Conclusion: God's revenge?

The rise of religious fundamentalism has attracted a great deal of attention which has intensified in the wake of 9/11. As the social base for a hegemonic project capable of challenging the common sense of global capitalism, it appears less convincing. The birth of the Islamic state did not manage to trigger a domino effect to the extent that it would have liked. In addition, while radical political Islam has the ideological might to challenge Western capitalism, the method of its challenge has reduced its potential to mobilize sustained popular support. The extreme form of Salafist jihadism has not been able to forge a successful partnership with Salafist Islamists in order to create a meaningful war of position. Likewise, Christianity and Hinduism may have appeared to respond to the 'immoral' consumerism that has accompanied globalization, but they often do so in a manner that engages with the principles of free market capitalism rather than opposing it.

What the respective religious movements have done is to create a set of strategic manoeuvres that have the potential to clash and create instabilities. This is not to argue that a 'clash of civilizations' is emerging or that an inevitable doomsday scenario will occur in the manner that Huntington argued. While radical Islam's main target of opposition might be the USA and what it sees as US-inspired Westernization, fundamentalist Christianity sees the Islamification of the Holy Land as its main threat. Finally, as we have seen, Hindutva views both Islamism and Christianity as external threats. All three defend their respective positions through a literal reading of scriptures. As these respective movements continue to expand across borders, so the potential for confrontation might grow. It is the results of and potential fallouts from such clashes which may have an effect on the wider stability of world order.

6 | THE AGE OF AUSTERITY

Criticism is something we can avoid easily by saying nothing, doing nothing, and being nothing (Aristotle)

The strength and viability of the three strands of hegemonic challenges to neoliberalism can be assessed in light of the financial crisis that has emerged in the last five or so years. The crisis should have allowed them to intensify their challenge to the common sense that neoliberalism relies upon. What has happened instead is that the weaknesses inherent within these challenges have been such that neoliberalism has sought to reinvent itself. By seeking to cut debt through reducing fiscal targets, states and governments, encouraged by business elites, are hoping that the market will restimulate growth. Debt relief has been seen as the first priority of states, which have stressed the importance of prudence during times of crisis. This has been intensified by the crisis of the euro and by the disciplining of failing states by the European Central Bank. What has become apparent is that neoliberalism is trying to reinvent its common sense in order to survive. The old logic that neoliberalism rests upon its ability to stimulate unparalleled growth has been replaced by a logic that sees crisis as a necessary part of the process of free market capitalism (Crouch 2011).

As a result, neoliberalism is reinventing itself by going on the defensive. Yet this defence has been made easier by the failure of alternative hegemonic challenges. Despite the crisis having stimulated a series of protests across society, the lack of a serious set of proposals resulting from this has meant that such protests have been dismissed. Whether the austerity measures can continue to fend off such attacks on a long-term basis is far more debatable. Also, as we shall examine in the next chapter, despite the lack of concrete alternative strategies for the overall governance of the global economy, the continued failure of the policies of austerity could mean that a structural change may emerge in the manner in which capitalism manages itself. Such a change could, for example, lead to wider geographical challenges that might threaten the global survival of neoliberalism and see its fall from grace. At present, however, the practice of 'austerity' is being utilized so that the neoliberal system can be maintained. Never before has Polanyi's concept of the 'market mentality' been quite so apt (Polanyi 1968: 3–77). Such has been the belief that the economy should remain free from intervention of any kind that austerity is a natural policy initiative during periods of crisis. In addition, a further message has been that the state needs to be more prudent during periods of boom, so that debt burdens can be avoided in the future. Questioning the overriding logic of the nature of the free market has been avoided by leading governments. Instead it has been presented as a sort of sacred cow, which must be preserved in order for the international political economy as we know it to survive. It has been the failure to move beyond an increasingly obsolete market mentality (to borrow precisely from Polanyi) which has prompted adherence to the need for austerity.

The financial crisis and the moment for change

In the aftermath of the credit crisis, there was a brief moment in which neoliberalism did appear to be on its final deathbed. When Alan Greenspan came up in front of Congress in late 2008 and admitted that the deregulatory free market philosophy that he practised exclusively during his spell as chairman of the Federal Reserve was in fact flawed, there was a widespread belief that we were witnessing a sea-change in the management of the global economy.[1] The talk of a new challenge to the primacy of deregulation was continued at the 2008 G8 summit in Washington when UK prime minister Gordon Brown called for a New Bretton Woods and his arguments were endorsed by both France's Nicolas Sarkozy and George W. Bush. These calls were continued in 2009 when Zhou Xiaochuan, governor of the People's Bank of China, argued that a global currency reserve of the sort that Keynes argued for in the 1940s should be initiated. Xiaochuan reminded us that the crisis of the dollar system was due to the fact that a currency cannot provide liquidity to world markets while at the same time maintaining its value as the reserve. This observation became universally known at the time as the Triffin dilemma and was seen to be one of the main obstacles to any future form of regulatory body upon similar lines. Yet the dollar was chosen by Harry Dexter White and his team ahead of the 'Bancor', which Keynes and his collaborator E. F. Schumacher two years previously had suggested should be the name of such a reserve (Keynes 1942a, 1942b; Schumacher 1943). Suggestions that an international reserve currency should be used as a response to the crisis furthered the idea that Keynes had in fact been correct all along and if Bretton Woods had been constructed in a manner that would have provided an independent regulatory process then the regulatory system would have survived for longer.

This brief and short-lived Keynesian revival followed the bailout process that occurred in the wake of the collapse of banks and financial institutions throughout 2008. The economic injections led many to assume that this was a clear departure from the logic of market governance. The return of Keynes was echoed in the economic sections of many influential media outlets and was perhaps epitomized by the biography of Keynes by Robert Skidelsky in 2009, in which he argues that recent events in the management of the crisis have vindicated his arguments (Skidelsky 2009). Yet the Keynesianism that was applied throughout such bailouts represents a different kind of Keynesianism to the one with which Keynes himself is associated. As Crouch and Gamble have argued, what neoliberalism really represents is a form of 'privatised Keynesianism' (Crouch 2011; Gamble 2009). Essentially, as argued in the first chapter, neoliberalism never managed to re-create the classical liberal form of laissez-faire economics whereby the state allowed the market to dictate entirely the results of production and social relations. Instead, states have used specific strategies to stimulate market growth. In doing so they encouraged banks and credit lenders to extend credit in order to maximize competition and extend a growth bubble. By doing this, the state encouraged institutional and individual debt, which, over time, became ingrained into everyday life and common sense. Thus, the bailouts served to allow this system to be recycled and to stay afloat.

The revival of Keynes was accompanied by the revival of Marx. Followers of both can claim to have been proved to be right over the nature of the crisis, yet both sets have been slow to mobilize support behind solutions to transform the nature of the global economy. As David Harvey excellently outlined in his now well-known speech at the Royal Society of Arts, the crisis has demonstrated how capitalism is defined through its internal contradictions of capital accumulation, of which crisis is a central feature (Harvey 2010). Optimism following the crisis was also seen in the World Social Forum in Belém in 2009.

Belém was seen as a vindication of the general message the Forum has been promulgating since its inception. Despite this, a concrete alternative that would realize the goals of socialism and democracy to replace the market system was not forwarded. The lack of direction from parties and organizations on the left in the immediate aftermath of the crisis also led to the moment for potential change being short lived. Despite this, criticisms, protests and opposition have occurred in abundance, especially in European countries that have become embroiled in the euro crisis. However, the fact that a coherent alternative has not materialized since the credit crisis emerged has allowed neoliberalism to regroup (metaphorically speaking) and restate its position. Such a position only goes to highlight the weakness of the left since the end of the Cold War in providing a challenging and a robust response to the management of the global economy.

Austerity: the new common sense?

Austerity is deemed both a necessity and a way of redirecting the cause of the crisis so that reckless fiscal spending is seen as the root cause. In the first instance, this saw a move from a position that held that global reform of some sort was a necessity to one that saw the crisis as a regrettable yet ultimately cyclical process of capitalism. To a certain degree this is accepting a position that is taken by economists ranging from Marx and Minsky through to Hayek, but without following their suggested solutions. They all argue, from different standpoints, that crisis is a feature of capitalist development, with each indicating different solutions for its management. Minsky argues that cycles of capital in a free market inevitably lead to an investment bubble caused by speculation that is impossible to sustain. Either regulation of some kind is brought in, or the cycle continues (Nesvetailova 2007). The way that austerity has been utilized suggests that while there is an acceptance that such bubbles are endemic within capitalist systems, the only regulations required are those that manage the systemic risk more carefully. In other words, the fault lies with the behaviour of the bankers and brokers who did not regulate the bubble or constrain their own behaviour. As property markets have burst before owing to similar volatile behaviour, within living memory (such as in the late 1980s in the UK, for example), then we are left with the reality that is aptly described by Marx as history repeating itself first as tragedy and secondly as farce (Marx 1967).

The reality of austerity, however, accords with another of Marx's statements. In the *Grundrisse* he commented that during times of crisis, it is the working classes which are financially disciplined (Marx 1993). This, to a degree, allows for the system to recycle and survive. What should be stressed, however, is that it is the survival of the market system or, for want of a better word, neoliberalism itself that is dependent on such discipline. It is from this position that the principles of austerity have been built. The necessity of austerity is backed by the belief that too much state spending had preceded it. This has certainly been a response from right of centre parties in Anglo-Saxon nations. The recent US Republican campaign has been dominated by arguments over cutbacks and how extensive these should be. Likewise, the Conservative–Liberal Democrat coalition in Britain has blamed the previous administration for excessive state spending and irresponsibly avoiding necessary cuts. Here we see how a set of common practices and assumptions is constructed in a manner which finds its way into the public consciousness. Gramsci's own studies on common sense show us how its formation can be built upon an opposing set of ideas that favour conservatism and continuity. When deconstructed, common sense thus appears as an 'ambiguous, contradictory and multiform concept' (Gramsci 1971: 423). Austerity acts in a manner that seeks to preserve continuity by constructing a set of principles and myths that on close inspection may appear contradictory, but are accepted as logical and coherent. For example, on questions of debt, the logistics of austerity for the state have been presented in the same manner as they would for individuals. If individuals and families run up debt, then the debt has to be repaid or consequences faced. The same logic must then be applied to governments and states. While this is beginning to find acceptance within some elements of society, such a comparison is, as Krugman argues, flawed (Krugman 2012). While Krugman might use media columns to counter acceptance of the comparison through deployment of economic facts – e.g. that successful and stable economies are historically those that contain a high percentage of debt or that state debt does not have the same accountability as individual debt – the logic is beginning to take hegemonic hold within certain states.

Recent studies comparing popular attitudes when the financial crisis originally hit and those pertaining five years on tend to back up the notion that austerity is beginning to be accepted. For example, in the

UK understanding of the crisis and responsibility for the consequent austerity measures has changed. While at one time a high percentage of people asked in opinion surveys blamed the financial system and in particular the behaviour of bankers and speculators, cuts are now increasingly blamed on the previous Labour government and its irresponsible spending (Stanley 2011). Perhaps even more telling are attitudes to austerity itself, with an increasing percentage believing that it is a necessity and something that needs to be accepted.

So what are the main assertions of the common sense of austerity and just how much purchase are they gaining? The first follows on from the question of necessity and the belief that governments have to cut certain public funds in order to break even. Yet this itself follows on from a wider belief that in crisis it is essential for financial institutions to be kept afloat at all costs. This has proved to be the most contested area in terms of hegemonic consent for a number of contrasting and contradictory reasons, with high levels of discontent expressed, particularly within the Eurozone, with crisis-hit states ceding sovereign control of fiscal policy in order to adapt to the European Central Bank's (ECB) financial austerity measures endorsed and supported by the German government. Added to that has been the bailing out of national banks within the Eurozone by bond-holders, who have insisted upon a stringent repayment conditionality. For citizens within such countries this requirement is hard to take. In places such as Greece and Portugal, the sovereign debt crisis has reached levels where new loans have been agreed alongside stiffer austerity measures. In Ireland, the fallout from the winding down of the notorious Anglo Irish Bank has seen successive Irish governments readjust annual fiscal budgets drastically in order to meet the repayment criteria of the bond-holders. Each of these instances has brought a backlash within civil society where the issue of necessity has been coupled with the realization that national economic sovereignty has been lost.

One way of attempting to smooth such concerns has been seen in Italy. Here, a governmental bond crisis has led to circumstances within the Italian government whereby austerity measures are seen as essential for reducing the debt burden. The administration led by Silvio Berlusconi was judged to have largely bypassed the economic restructuring that was needed in order to meet repayment demands. The new administration led by Mario Monti has underlined the necessity of austerity by working alongside governments and institutions in order to produce a far more realistic restructuring plan than had previously been suggested. Any additional EU bailout would have to be on condition of a sharp reduction in fiscal spending in other sections of the economy. Here we see another tactic in the attempt to embed the common sense of austerity. As an economic powerhouse in its own right, Italy is essential to the sustainability of the global economy and the future of the euro. As such, the message being stressed within Italy and the global economic community is that if Italy cannot meet the requirements needed in such a restructuring then there would be serious repercussions across the Eurozone as a whole. Italy has been seen as one of the 'big three' states that dominate the European Financial Stability Fund, created to assist states to meet their targets in light of the crisis. More importantly, it appeared, alongside France and Germany, as one of the leading drivers of economic integration. While it might be manageable for a smaller economy within the Eurozone to drop out, it would be catastrophic for the sustainability of the euro itself if Italy were to pursue a similar course. Thus, in the case of Italy, austerity is being understood not just as a necessity but as the only possible option. It would therefore be irresponsible not to embark upon substantial economic rigidity in order to allow the euro and the global economic system to survive.

The principles of necessity and the harsh realities of statements such as 'there is no alternative but austerity' and 'in evading it the situation is being made worse' highlight a more obvious logic that underlines the common sense of austerity. That is the conviction that it is the market and the private sector which drive economic productivity and growth. The tenets of neoliberalism have made such an impression on the manner in which the economy functions that when practitioners and politicians have looked at ways in which reform could occur they seem unable to move beyond the popular common-sense perception that the private sector remains the central wealth-generating sector and should be encouraged as much as possible. It is this logic which has traditionally been embedded within conservative and centre-right parties, but since the end of the Cold War it has slowly been accepted throughout mainstream political culture. Thus, from the collapse of communism, the 'end of history' or the 'victory of capitalism' that I outlined in the first chapter, a common sense emerged, aided by the culture of consumerism and popular media outlets,[2] whereby the private sector is seen as the vital cog in economic and human development. The consequence of this is that during a crisis it is the public sector which is seen as expendable. As the private sector is the priority in terms of revival, then its restimulation is the key to economic recovery. The narrative here is that the private sector requires less regulation of business practices in order to give enterprises a 'chance to survive' and stimulate competition. In addition, it is the private sector which serves as both the wealth creator and the source of job creation. Therefore any attempt to regulate the practices of such ventures should be avoided.

It is on the principles of private competition that the logic behind austerity rests. As Liam Stanley has recently outlined, it has been through the acceptance of narratives such as the need to 'balance the books' and on demonization of 'ending reckless borrowing and spending' that it bases its common sense. Alongside this Keynesian crisis management is dismissed as 'irresponsible' and similar to 'extending an overdraft'. Equally telling is that the extent of the other components of external debt – namely individual, consumer and property debt – is increasingly being ignored (Stanley 2011: 7). What began in 2008 as a crisis known as the 'credit crunch', when the finger of irresponsibility was pointed at banks facilitating large mortgages and at the culture of personal credit debt, has now been transformed into a 'financial crisis' where the blame seems to lie solely with the state. Even the name, it seems, has been altered to account for the changing interpretations of the nature of the slump. Yet such a position has also attracted a number of more fundamental market positions that have criticized mainstream approaches for their part in the management of the crisis and the use of debt in the first instance. Such criticisms were highlighted by Andrew Gamble in his account of the crisis. He outlines the differences between 'market fundamentalists' over the ways in which financial crisis should be managed. On the one hand there are those who believe that the state's main purpose is to get the market up and running again, and if that requires intervention then intervention should take place, provided its overall purpose is to balance the books and restore a functioning market economy (Gamble 2009: 144–5). Yet there are others who take a position that is rooted far more in market anarchy. Here, the blame lies not just with state spending but with over-regulation of the economy by banks and financial regulators. One of the obvious targets in the USA was the Federal Reserve, which interfered with interest rates during the boom years and has a history of attracting criticism that it has operated as a way of promoting the interests of an elitist few. Here, the arguments follow a body of extreme thinking behind the idea of anarcho-capitalism promulgated by Murray Rothbard, which states that central banks need to be abolished as they lead to the promotion of borrowing or credit bubbles (Rothbard 1994).

Hayek and the Austrian School can be seen as endorsing both the above claims. For example, Hayek believed that the state's main role was to ensure the smooth operation of the market, to provide a basis for sound money and to restore confidence in the economy (Gamble and Payne 1996). Conversely, those who are closer to the ideals of anarcho-capitalism believe that the warnings about the unsustainability of credit expansion can be seen in Von Mises and Hayek's development of the Austrian business cycle theory (Von Mises 1934 [1912]; Hayek 1931). These works explicitly demonstrate that low interest rates applied by central banks create a surge in credit and debt. More importantly, they undermine the markets' attempt to form a natural equilibrium so that they can function properly. As Hayek was also at pains to stress, a market society does throw up winners and losers, and for it to preserve the libertarian effect that it desires, this must be maintained without exceptions. Under this logic, governmental bailouts should be resisted as they reward institutions that fail when it is their own ill-discipline which has brought them to that point. Therefore, banks should suffer the same consequences of failure as other business. In the long term this would force such institutions to reduce potential risk and act more responsibly. It has been through this new understanding of market fundamentalism that a new body of criticism has emerged which aims to restate the importance of the free market and low taxation in opposition to bailout policies.

The Tea Party and fellow travellers

The growth of the Tea Party following the financial crisis has attracted no end of media attention. Rather than a movement geared towards challenging the rhetoric of neoliberal capitalism, the reverse has been the case. Namely, the Tea Party believes that the principles of the free market and of libertarianism have been threatened by financial bailouts and the absence of draconian welfare cuts. The

Tea Party emerged as a response to precisely what was seen as state intervention in the market, in the manner and tradition of Murray Rothbard's interpretation of Austrian School economics (Rothbard 1994). This has been popularized through the belief that the economic bailouts that were agreed by successive administrations were against the spirit of the American Revolution. Fuelled by new media, the Tea Party emerged as a group that organized protests against the financial bailouts, excessive federal regulation of small business and taxation at the beginning of 2009. By the end of the year, the protests were extended to include new welfare measures being proposed by the Obama administration, which included health reform. By mixing a more concentrated form of market ideology with a dose of American patriotism, the Tea Party manages to embed some of the reactionary populism that was discussed in Chapter 4 within a neoliberal discourse.

While seen as a grassroots organization, the Tea Party lacks a unified structure and appears to be largely an umbrella movement that incorporates a wide set of socially conservative and economic-ally liberal campaigns. Therefore, much of the social make-up of participants within the movement is hard to ascertain. Of the media outlets that have tried to map the demographics and nature of support of the Tea Party, many have been unable to make firm statements about its social configuration. If anything, polls have found that the Tea Party is generally a reasonable reflection of US society in terms of demographics, gender and education, while the disparities in race are evident but not particularly striking (Gallup 2010).[3] The distinction, as might be expected, lies in where they see themselves politically, with an overwhelming majority associating themselves with the conservative right. Yet there are also very definite divisions in both regional representations of the movement and the interpretation of libertarianism. While there are firm views on socially conservative issues such as abortion, homosexuality and crime, there is debate on how these issues should be regulated. As much of the Tea Party movement emerged as a means of reviving adherence to the constitu-tion in American society, many reaffirm the belief that such decisions should be determined at state rather than federal level.

While the Tea Party has no distinct political home in its own right, a number of influential organizations have emerged to lead and direct some of its campaigns. These include the Tea Party Patriots, Americans for Prosperity and Patriot Action Network, as well as business-friendly groups and maverick individuals that have combined to set up the regional, state and national convention. As such a wide organization, it remains difficult to see what unites it and what definite goals and commitments unify it. The Patriot Action Network, for example, identifies four points as being core Tea Party principles. These being limited government, fiscal responsibility, constitutional governance and free markets (Patriot Action 2011). This is a view shared by groups such as the Tea Party Patriots and the Tea Party Nation, which urge any candidate that stands on the Tea Party platform to vote against tax increases and support a 10 per cent reduction in spending at every level. The website that provides contacts for local groups, on the other hand, seems to extend these commitments to '15 non-negotiable core beliefs'. These include a commitment to family values, gun ownership, domestic employment and English being retained as the official language of the USA (Tea Party 2011). The Tea Party has also witnessed the emergence of certain individuals, such as Christine O'Donnell, Dick Amery and the billionaire philanthropist brothers David and Charles Koch. The protests and events that have been associated with the Tea Party have also given Republican politicians a platform for greater support. For example, Sarah Palin, Michelle Bachman, Newt Gingrich and Rick Perry have all courted and promised to endorse key Tea Party principles while in political office.

The Tea Party movement has thus served to restore key neoliberal principles to the contemporary political agenda and has provided a counter-argument to the widespread bailouts by favouring a market fundamentalist position. Yet has this been solely an American experience? Has the election of Obama, alongside a commitment to wider public health access, provided a unique American backlash whereby opposition is framed around the assumption that too much regulation and state spending are eroding liberty and adding to the debt burden? Or has this position spread to other parts of the world, especially across the Atlantic? The answer to this is inconclusive. With the euro crisis ongoing, it is difficult to make a strong case for similar forms of support, although, as mentioned above, the case for austerity is being made. Yet it would take a great deal more persuasion within Europe to argue that even greater cuts should be made than those already being suggested. It might appeal to those anti-immigration political movements on the far right that have sought to embed market economics and welfare chauvinism within forms of national-populism (see Chapter 4).

In the European Parliament the Europe of Freedom and Democracy group has affiliated members that seem to endorse the position. The Eurosceptic group consists of a number of contrasting and unlikely bedfellows, but the two dominant groups have leanings towards market populism. Politicians in Italy's Lega Nord have used Monti's new government to construct a fresh attack on the execution of the proposed austerity measures, based primarily around the popular principle of low taxation. UKIP, the other dominant group, has been more active in trying to establish connections with the movements on the other side of the Atlantic. Openly declaring itself as the 'British Tea Party' on both American and British news outlets, UKIP has long stressed its commitment to free markets and less government intervention in the economy as a way of distinguishing itself from the far and reactionary right. With the growth of the Tea Party in the USA, UKIP has been quick to draw out similarities. Both emerged from the dissatisfaction with catch-all conservative parties, both locate themselves within the Hayekian tradition and both are unequivocal in their belief that regulation and taxation hinder liberty. Where the Tea Party points to federal government as hindering this liberty, UKIP points to the EU, and both have sought to question mainstream positions on environmental degeneration by arguing strongly against international regulation. It is through these positions that UKIP, along with individuals who have remained on the Eurosceptic right wing of the UK Conservative Party (such as Daniel Hannon), has made firm attempts to align itself, at least in spirit, with the Tea Party movement.

In terms of leadership, this new brand of market populism has seen a number of what we can term traditional and organic intellectuals. The numerous traditional intellectuals from the right have reaffirmed their belief in marketization and have referred to both free market economists and constitutional libertarians. Organic intellectuals have looked to re-emphasize popular themes such as low taxation, the erosion of the small businessman or the 'American dream' and the attack on the constitution, and these have been favourite rallying calls. The organization of the Tea Party has also allowed for organic intellectuals to become prominent through the staging of conventions at the local, municipal and state levels. In addition, popular books and leaflets, such as Meckler and Martin's *Tea Party Patriots* or Farah's *Tea Party Manifesto*, have endorsed these principles and campaigns. Yet no one has managed to attract as much attention or has been as symbolically central to the movement as the veteran libertarian politician Ron Paul, who has been called the 'Godfather' of the movement.

Ron Paul: a neoliberal prince? The emergence of Ron Paul as both a defender of liberty and a supporter of free market economics has been one that has surprised a number of commentators within the USA. He is a long-serving Texas congressman who became highly influenced by *The Road to Serfdom* and the Austrian School while a medical student. This was reinforced by the collapse of the dollar system, as Paul argued that a fiat system, whereby currency is not tied to a commodity but printed at will, would inevitably lead to debt. Yet he was a keen member of the new right and supporter of Reagan's move to reduce the burden of government in the early 1980s, but left the administration owing to its failure to control the federal budget and rising debt. He stood on the Libertarian Party ticket in the presidential election of 1988, and even supported the protectionist Pat Buchanan ahead of George Bush Sr in 1992, before returning to the Republican fold in Congress in 1997. With the onset of the financial crisis, Paul, who had by this time long since been considered a relic from the past, resurfaced in 2008 with his bid for the Republican nomination for the presidency. The 2008 campaign saw his brand of market populism slowly finding a niche just as the financial bailouts were being agreed and a new era of financial regulation was being talked up. The success of the Tea Party partly had its roots in Paul's presidential campaigns and following the publication of *The Revolution: A Manifesto* in 2008. His subsequent popularity, which has led to him standing again in 2012, has seen him appeal to a wide section of the American public, propelling him to almost cult status among many.

So how have the utterings of a seventy-something managed to find popular support within US civil society and as a result inadvertently defended neoliberal ideology? Paul has managed (again inadvertently) to find a political solution that blends market idealism with the principles that were enshrined within the American constitution. For example, he dismisses notions that the constitution is adaptable to historical change and refers to George Orwell's parody of the chief pigs adapting the principles that are put down after the revolution in *Animal Farm* to suit their purpose in order to highlight this (Paul 2008: 49). Against neoconservative expansionism, he also has argued for US withdrawal in regions such as the Middle East, and is opposed to future campaigns on the basis that interventionism was against the ideals of the founding fathers. Paul also stresses that he is opposed to the Pat Buchanan/John Birch Society isolationists, as he argues for the primacy of free trade and bilateral relationships between similar-minded liberal democracies. More interestingly, he is also opposed to a special relationship with Israel and with any form of foreign aid for military and economic purposes. Such issues have often placed him at odds with the majority of Republicans and conservatives. This has also been the case with some of his social issues, such as his rather ambiguous stance on the death penalty, which, in recent years, he has seemed to ethically oppose. Despite this, he has won support within the Tea Party owing to his conviction that such issues should be resolved at the local level of the state, rather than at federal level.

It has been Paul's ability to frame his arguments around his own interpretation of the founding fathers of the USA which has generated popular support. His economic policies operate in the same vein. Influenced by a wide range of market fundamentalists, including Cobden and the laissez-faire pragmatists of Victorian England along with the more obvious names of Hayek, Von Mises and Rothbard, Paul has attempted to use the same populist rhetoric that was implicit in the economic arguments of Reagan and Thatcher. This influence is seen in his proposals for change, which include an endorsement of the nineteenth-century gold standard, a huge reduction in welfare spending and a similar reduction in governmental regulation. Quoting the Von Mises argument that state intervention in the economy provides a spiral effect whereby more and more regulation is needed to supervise such a process, he argues that less governance is required to make the market work. Thus bodies such as the World Bank and the World Trade Organization actually hinder the free market as they appear to act as intergovernmental entities (ibid.: 88–97). Finally, in the spirit of Murray Rothbard, Paul has called for an end to the US Federal Reserve, arguing that its abolition would allow the US economy to flourish through market rule alone (Paul 2009: 7–8).

The campaigns of Ron Paul lead us to draw a number of interesting conclusions. First, through the Tea Party movement, populist campaigns such as those that attack international institutionalism and which had previously been associated with nationalist and protectionist ideologies have now been placed within a market context. Secondly, while the libertarian argument that Paul makes has not succeeded in winning over the neoconservative majority in the Republican Party, his presence has allowed the market fundamentalist position to flourish as a whole. Paul, alongside other Tea Party favourites such as Bachman, has pledged tax cuts and further deregulation as against the bailouts used by successive administrations. Thus, from the ashes of the financial crisis, we have witnessed the birth of a popular movement that has aimed to resist any form of international financial regulation or reform suggested at the start of the crisis. Instead, its adherents have sought to defend the principles of unregulated free market capitalism.

From austerity to growth?

If the Tea Party represented the endorsement of austerity from the political right, then the political left have responded by stressing the need to reorient the objectives of austerity so that they are geared far more towards regenerating economic growth. The election of François Hollande in the French presidential elections in 2012 has suggested that a sea-change of sorts has occurred in the way austerity is being approached. With the euro crisis not reaching a stable conclusion following the conditional bailouts that were insisted upon by Angela Merkel, Hollande swept to victory in France with a mandate that sought to challenge the way in which the economic crisis was being managed within the European heartland. The months leading up to Hollande's election success saw a number of forms of discontent across the Eurozone, with demonstrations throughout Europe over the conditions for the bailouts set by the ECB reaching new levels. The implosion of the political centre in Greece that became evident by the time of the May election, and the slump in support for Merkel's Christian Democrats, added to the growing unease that the route of austerity taken by the Eurozone will not lead to a long-term solution to the crisis.

Hollande emerged from his campaign with a mandate that included a pledge to endorse a form of international 'Robin Hood' tax, a tightening of income tax to reduce the potential for loopholes for tax avoiders, and to construct a new Franco-German alliance that would serve to protect public services. The aftermath of his victory has seen calls for a more institutional solution to the sovereign debt problem within the Eurozone, such as the expansion of the ECB's Security Markets Programme (SMP), which aims to stabilize debt difficulties within the PIIGS through issuance of bonds. While this interventionist move has led to some change in terms of the approach to the sovereign debt crisis within Europe, the change seems to boil down to embracing 'growth' rather than 'austerity'. In other words, austerity has come to mean a process whereby governments do nothing but cut spending. It is this which has become unpopular, because it lacks any form of an 'endgame' or a strategy that looks to economic growth. Therefore, austerity is effective only if it is challenged through a wider strategy geared towards economic growth and recovery.

Hollande's election soundbites were dominated by the idea that austerity in its present form isn't working and that he favoured a new type of crisis management geared towards growth and recovery. The use of 'growth' as a buzz word was designed to distinguish the idea of pursuing economic growth from the idea that a reduction in debt through cuts to state spending can relieve the burden on its own. While this was designed to demonstrate a significant difference in the way in which economic policy was understood, and to pave the way for some of the ideas of the left to gain momentum, a closer look at the notion of 'growth' suggests that the change is based not on greater intervention in the economy, but on ways in which the market might reignite wider growth. This would suggest that what is emerging is a wider dispute over how austerity as a whole should be utilized. On the one side, those on the libertarian right argue that state debt is dramatically reduced through cuts to state spending and adoption of a greater concentration of market forces so that the economy floats unregulated to form its own winners and losers, thus providing an equilibrium that will allow for a more effective market economy. On the other, there is a conviction that state and institutional bodies should intervene to find ways whereby the global market economy can be restimulated. If the market fundamentalism of the Tea Party reflects the first position, then the 'growth' initiative that seems to be emerging in light of the euro crisis seems to represent the second.

This is not to suggest that Hollande's victory, coupled with the increased discontent towards austerity measures that have become associated with Merkel, has not resulted in a challenge to the processes of neoliberalism. To a degree, Hollande's victory underlines the credentials of a social Europe that has long sought to counter the market excess of neoliberalism (Clift 2003). At present, however, the political direction suggested by those who stressed the importance of growth does not amount to a radical challenge to the current neoliberal status quo. Here, it seems clear that the narrative of austerity isn't being contested per se, but rather that debates are emerging over what type of austerity is necessary for economic revival. From this, we can perhaps suggest that the defensive narrative that has emerged since the crisis regarding neoliberalism may be seen to be working. For both positions (for the Tea Party on one side and for those that favour a more directed and cautious approach to spending cuts) the objective appears not to be geared towards overhauling the market system but towards fixing it. If anything, what has been noticeable is that it is the term 'austerity' itself which is beginning to become unpopular, rather than the common sense that has begun to emerge from it. The new response that has emerged within parts of Europe and has recently been associated with Hollande's commitment to 'growth' seems to be one in which the main bone of contention is undirected forms of austerity, rather than the nature of the global economy as a whole. Recent divisions have emerged between Hollande and Monti, uniting to favour a more directed commitment to growth, and the more traditional centre-right, including Merkel, stressing the primacy of fiscal discipline.

Conclusion: neoliberalism on the defensive?

Despite the input of the Tea Party in the USA, the policies of austerity have generally been treated by governments as a necessary response to the crisis and as unavoidable measures. In this sense they appear to be a defensive mechanism in terms of the wider principles of neoliberalism. Yet the lack of an alternative to these measures, at least at governmental level, has allowed this defensive mechanism to construct its own forms of logic and common sense. For example, it has allowed positions to develop that have questioned the levels of austerity and put forth strategies to reinvigorate the global market. It has also left space for a market fundamentalist position to gain a niche. Both developments will only serve to strengthen this defence as debates threaten to turn from questioning the overall validity of the neoliberal system to what form it should take. Such moves would give neoliberalism a new lease of life and provide even more ammunition to those who argue that there is no alternative. However, across Europe as well as in parts of Latin America and Asia, the argument that the crisis occurred because of too much regulation is a non-starter. The financial cuts have instead been met with growing resentment as governments have tried to present them as a necessity, whether by seeking to blame previous overspending or by arguing that no other way out exists. While this might have gone some way to legitimizing the cuts, the huge discontent that remains evident within the public sector has shown that this legitimacy has got a long way to go to gain some degree of acceptance.

While neoliberalism has sought to use austerity as a method of staving off structural change, many are referring to the current era as one which will increasingly appear 'post-neoliberal' in character. These claims do not suggest that the present order is no longer operating according to the principles of neoliberalism, but that neoliberalism as a model for economic growth has run its course. As I will explain in the next chapter, many look to China and the rise of what have become known as the BRIC countries (Brazil, Russia, India and China) and the use of what has increasingly been referred to as 'state capitalism' (Beeson 2009). Similar arguments are used concerning the sustainability of neoliberalism. Many have raised doubts about whether continued austerity measures can actually restimulate market growth and indeed whether they can have the desired effect of staving off debt. Without a regulatory framework in place to tackle credit and borrowing, it seems that certain governments appear content to allow the market to be restimulated by the same means as before. In this instance, they look to bypass the question of widespread reform by waiting for the market to pick up and allowing the private sector the conditions for market revival by cutting public funds. Yet it has not just been Keynesians such as Paul Krugman who have highlighted the dangers of pulling money out of an economy in order to attempt to redress debt. Even the World Bank, the institution synonymous with structural adjustment, has criticized the austerity measures and argued that they are becoming counterproductive. Despite not giving any firm guidelines over whether alternatives were required in economic governance, the World Bank, the IMF and the World Trade Organization (among others) have nonetheless called upon leading governments to tone down austerity measures and look for other means to create growth and stimulate the market (Elliott 2012). The general concern here is that the longer austerity measures continue, the more damage they will do if the market doesn't pick up as intended.

Why, we have to ask, have the alternative hegemonic projects that were outlined in previous chapters not succeeded in advancing their respective causes during this time? As we have seen in this chapter, some nationalist and populist sentiment has been used as a means to form fresh anti-welfare market critiques. This has added to the fragmentation that has been inherent within right-wing movements in terms of their economic coherence. As for the campaigns for transformation at the international level, the Occupy movement has at least appeared to be true to its intentions, despite the lack of a clear programme. This is a point that has even been made by notable conservative commentators, who have suggested that, unlike the Tea Party, the movement is not rife with contradictions in terms of what it claims to represent (Fukuyama 2012). However, we are still left questioning why the campaigns to reform and regulate the international economic system have not made the headway that they might have been expected to in light of the crisis. Some might claim that they are indeed looking to such reforms as a means of instigating change. While Xiaochuan's proposals and the Bancor may have been wishful thinking in terms of it becoming a reality in the near future, French president Sarkozy made a pledge to introduce the Tobin tax as part of his re-election campaign. While this would not be implemented at the rate originally intended,[4] it would act as a benchmark for other states to follow. Yet such politically motivated moves are not going to result in a change to the reality of the global political economy in its post-crisis era. Despite its fragility, neoliberalism seems capable of defending itself from such solitary moves.

7 | NEOLIBERALISM AND POTENTIAL TRANSFORMATION

I'm a pessimist because of intelligence, but an optimist because of will (Antonio Gramsci, letter to his brother Carlo, 1929)

As we have seen, there can be no doubt that if we were to analyse the brief history of neoliberalism as a working formula, we would have to conclude that it is now on the defensive. We have also seen that this defence has been aided by the shortcomings of alternative forms of governance, despite the increase in resistance and dissatisfaction. This final chapter seeks to look at the potential transformation that might occur to economic global governance in the future. There are a number of scenarios to examine. First, if a new Prince cannot be formed through state/civil construction of an ideological alternative, then it might emerge through the formation of new states which would favour a different approach to neoliberalism. Secondly, many authors have tried to construct their own visions and manifestos to illustrate how neoliberal capitalism can be transformed and replaced. These contain a wide selection of ideas and suggestions for practical strategies for change. Some have argued for forms of multicultural democracy or global institutional democracy (Tannsjo 2008) or for global financial reform (Brassett 2010). Others have followed the spirit of Gill's 'Postmodern Prince' and tentatively sketched ideas for post-national alternatives (Burbach 2001). Then there are those who make the argument that we should return to more familiar territory when thinking about transformation and argue for a return to socialist values and as such a return to the alternative of planned economies (Callinicos 2003).

While all these contributions make serious attempts to put alternatives on a concrete base, there are also far too many academic books and articles that provide criticisms of the present system, but add only a last chapter or concluding statement on what form such alternatives should take. As a result there have been several suggestions as to 'what is needed' or 'what should be done', but they have often been tentatively and vaguely placed at the end as if to make some sort of final gesture towards the need for change. As I have outlined the shortcomings of potential alternative challenges, my analysis will be open to considerable criticism if I do not provide some form of direction regarding what a successful hegemonic challenge might need to do in order to seriously threaten the contemporary order. Such a challenge can only really emerge through a broad set of coalitions that are geared towards contesting and challenging the very common sense that neoliberalism rests upon. As we have seen, one of the key successes of neoliberalism is that it has developed a whole set of common assumptions based upon the belief that the free market is the key to generating economic growth, and during times of crisis, an economic recovery depends upon the maintenance of a competitive market. At the beginning of the crisis these assumptions were in serious threat of being tested, but the onset of austerity and the 'need' to reduce debt have restored some stability to these assumptions. Any successful challenge would thus need to contest these assumptions constantly by promoting a fresh set of proposals that are popularized across a wide cross-section of society.

Neoliberalism versus state capitalism?

One of the major consequences of the fallout of the financial crisis has been the realization that China has emerged as a significant economic actor on the global stage. Its position as the largest fiscal surplus country has led to several states prioritizing China as a potential investor. Its prominence has been even more notable in light of the financial bailouts that propelled the central bank of China into the position of the largest foreign holder of US debt. Its remarkable economic rise has seen it become the second-largest economy in the world, with its growth rates being such that it has the potential to overtake the USA within the next few decades. Perhaps more important is its potential as a leader of developing countries. Its role within the G77 and the G20 development bloc has been increasingly prominent, and its continued investment in the developing world has certainly provided a rivalry to the USA in terms of influence.

As a result of the emergence of China, particularly as an influence over the developing world, many have suggested that the Chinese model of capitalism offers a significantly different model of economic development to neoliberalism. In response to the neoliberal

Washington Consensus, the term Beijing Consensus has been applied to describe China's version of capitalism. The highly controlled and managed 'post-Listian' approach, whereby the middle classes do not push for greater liberalization from the state but favour a mix of state and private enterprise, contrasts with the market-led systems in the West (Strange 2011; Beeson 2009). To a degree this observation follows those who have argued for many years that greater comparative studies are needed when looking into the characteristics of national economies (Hall and Soskice 2001). In France, where inequality has decreased since the Gaullist days of huge disparities, it has long been fashionable to regard neoliberalism as an Anglo-Saxon phenomenon which they have sought to resist. Yet, as I outlined in Chapter 1, the reality of neoliberal globalization has been such that the move to market solutions has increasingly limited any significant national challenge from continental Europe, a situation which at present seems to be continuing given the favoured austerity measures within the Eurozone. Conversely, China has been supported in some of its endeavours by Brazil, Russia and India, forming a quartet that is considered to comprise the big four emerging powerhouses, often referred to as the BRIC nations.

The BRIC nations have in recent years all pursued policies that have suggested that they could challenge the long-term hegemony of neoliberalism. The Doha Round of trade negotiations at the WTO came to an abrupt halt in 2008 over the failure to agree safeguards over special tariffs for indigenous or low-wage farmers in the event of an import surge or drastic alteration in market prices. This itself ultimately led to a stalemate between the USA and India, but the collapse illustrated the new-found influence that such states had in multilateral talks. The final accession of Russia to the WTO has also brought suggestions that the more managed market economies could provide a future alternative to their neoliberal counterpart. Finally, as we have seen in Chapter 3, the emergence of Brazil has been complemented by a resurgence of regional opposition to neoliberalism within Latin America. This has led to more speculation over whether the continent can develop a form of social developmental capitalism with Brazil at the helm (Beasley-Murray et al. 2009). As a bloc, the region could be the new guardian of the developing world, with enormous consequences for the future form of multinational investment.

So just how viable is the possibility of the BRIC countries forming an alternative model of capitalism? There are a number of issues here which need to be discussed before we can suggest such a development. First, while the BRICs have used the state far more to promote their own economic development, this has been in order to find an effective way to integrate into the global economy. The methods of integration might vary but have ultimately been based on maximizing what assets they have to use in the global market. Thus India and China have positioned themselves as manufacturing powerhouses and have looked to globalize their economies by attracting multinational investment and FDI (Downes 2009: 102). As such they have emerged as semi-peripheral states that have become dependent upon economic activity generated in the West for their expansion. This is not to say that such states could not eventually contest the make-up of the global system as a whole, however. Indeed, much analysis of the nature of semi-peripheral states points to how they often appear at the forefront of change, pointing to instances such as the Russian Revolution, where a reaction against the existing system led to its transformation (Worth and Moore 2009). As neither firmly entrenched within the dominant ideology of leading states, nor strong enough to challenge their position, the BRIC states have the capability of leading such peripheral regions towards a potential challenge. However, unlike with the revolutionary or ideologically challenging positions of the past, the success of the BRIC economies has come through working within the processes of the global economy itself. Furthermore, when such states have reacted against the practices of the global economy in the past, the intended results have not materialized. For example, protectionist measures under the banner of 'import substitution' in parts of South America and South Asia largely failed to deliver. Far from creating domestic alternatives in order to buck dominant trends within the international economy, the experience left a legacy of debt that was to pave the way for the structural adjustment reforms of the following decades.[1]

Following on from this, it remains to be seen whether the more managed economies of India, China and (increasingly) Russia are offering any alternative. The forms of economic liberalization that have taken place in India and China have occurred owing to strategic integration into the global economy, whereby both have responded to the wider process of financial globalization by internationalizing their domestic economies accordingly. The colossal increases of FDI into both states in the last two decades, and the transformation of their workforces in order to attract interest from multinational corporations, have been the cornerstone of the economic growth. This is a trend that has continued in Russia. There, the rush towards price liberalization and privatization in the aftermath of the split-up of the Soviet Union led to the notorious oligarchic takeover of the economy. This in turn led to a reduction in investment and saw the Russian economy stagnate until the end of the century. Its revival under Putin was marked by state-managed market reforms that have led to an increase in FDI over the last decade. Again, the intention here was to open up Russia's economy in a way that avoided the potential instabilities that occur under concentrated free market reform, and allow the state to provide a role as a sort of a watchdog for wider integration (Putin 2001). The question here remains whether the types of state-managed capitalism favoured by such emerging powers have stemmed from a desire to distinguish themselves from the more market-based authentic neoliberal ones favoured by more developed powers, or whether such an approach has been utilized in order to engage with the very hegemonic global practices that have been facilitated by the same neoliberal model. Of particular interest here is the role that multinational corporations have played in creating the demand for manufacturing labour in China and India, and how they have responded to meet such demand. The increased levels of skilled and semi-skilled workers coupled with an ever increasing flexible labour market have proved ideal conditions for multinational corporations to prosper.

Another argument made with regard to the emergence of a competing model of capitalism has emerged from South America. As outlined in Chapter 3, the emergence of the left in the continent has led to a collective belief within the region that the era of neoliberalism has passed and that a fresh, more socially inclusive form of political economy is beginning to be fashioned. In South America, the neoliberal period was associated with structural adjustment and the need to contain the debt crisis. It is also identified with American-friendly governments and with figures such as Sánchez de Lozada and Caldera (the predecessors of Morales and Chávez respectively). More symbolically, it is associated with the dictatorships that provided the initial laboratories for the neoliberal experiment (see Chapter 1). The notion of 'post-neoliberalism' has become popular in light of recent developments on the continent. The term has often been associated with a region-wide process that focuses upon export-led economies that prioritize social spending and a reduction in inequality (Grugel and Riggirozzi 2012). Both symbolically and in real terms this was to indicate a significant change in the direction of governance from the era of privatization and market reform. Inequality has decreased since the turn of the century, yet the rate of this decrease has perhaps not been as marked as one might expect and has largely been exaggerated owing to the preceding fallout from Argentina's debt default. Other studies have argued that in certain states, such as Brazil and Chile, there has been a more profound drop in equality than in others. Both countries have, as mentioned in Chapter 3, taken a more internationalist approach to development than, for example, Argentina, Venezuela and Bolivia, which are often considered populist and have not demonstrated so great a decrease in inequality (Mcleod and Lustig 2011). In addition, of all the semi-peripheral regions of the world, South America was perhaps as marked as any in being defined through its inequality. The improvements made during this so-called post-neoliberal turn may have been noticeable and played up by respective governments, but the region still remains characterized by its huge inequalities despite recent developments.

Neoliberalism versus left nationalism?

The idea of state capitalism revolves to a considerable extent around the principles of neo-mercantilism and, to a lesser extent, elements of Keynesianism. A left nationalist approach is one where the state plays a substantial role in organizing the economy in the belief that its management should be coordinated at a national level. The central argument here is that the state is the most effective channel for regulation and wealth redistribution. Left nationalism has a long and notable history and has been seen in the mixed economies of the post-war era in Europe (particularly in Scandinavia and the UK), in post-colonial forms of socialism and in forms of Soviet-inspired state socialism (Nairn 2005; Dunphy 2004; Lane 1996). Indeed, the national political economy form of Keynesianism that was embraced by the majority of social democratic political parties within the Western world became a notable feature of politics up to the neoliberal era. In addition, there has long been debate between those who favour a national-first approach and believe in a form of 'progressive nationalism' (Nimni 1985; Munck 1986, 2010; Calhoun 1997) and those who are more wary of it as a model or are indeed sceptical of such a process existing (Archibugi and Held 1995; Hardt and Negri 2000; Radice 2000; Ryan and Worth 2010). During times of crisis it might appear logical to assume that states might seek to look at greater intervention in order to counter the negative effects of market collapse.

Certainly there have been those who have suggested that the financial crisis will bring about a change in the way in which the global financial system is organized, with a greater role for state intervention and regulation (Germain 2010). Left nationalism could emerge again as a result. There has also been a precedent here. The import substitution form of protectionism that was practised by the Latin American states took its cue from the idea of left nationalism – namely, that the most effective way of challenging the inequalities within the international capitalist system was to shut oneself off from the system and put in place national regulatory restraints in order to redress national inequalities (Frank 1966). Left or 'progressive' nationalism can also be used both as a strategy for those within the camp of 'progressive internationalism' and as a way of challenging the chauvinistic or populist nationalism of the far right with an enlightened form. While this might appear contradictory, it should be remembered that many of those involved in the social forums are involved in supporting national liberation movements which favour forms of left nationalism. Indeed, as many have also argued, being 'internationalist' and 'nationalist' at the same time isn't necessarily a contradiction. If states are geared towards the mutual development of social democracy within their respective territories, then solidarity at a mutual level can exist (Gall 2009). Therefore it might be assumed that one of the more practical ways of contesting neoliberalism would be to garner support for the re-establishment of national social democratic or socialist projects.

Yet, with the exception of some traditional left parties (particularly in parts of Scandinavia) and subregional or national independence parties (such as the many Celtic independence parties, Sinn Fein in Ireland and the Catalan and Basque movements in Spain), there has been a distinct lack of interest in constructing forms of national left strategies. Even within the Euro-sceptic left, who have traditionally maintained the importance of public ownership and nationalization, there have been questions over whether this traditional statist form of social democracy is viable in the contemporary era of globalization (Dunphy 2004). Certainly the growth of material cosmopolitanism and global civil society (see Chapter 3) has left any intellectual platform for left nationalist renewal in retreat. Again, in light of moves towards greater regulation, it might emerge in parts of the post-communist world and in East Asia, either to counteract the ideals of state capitalism or indeed to complement forms of state capitalism as a national response. Yet the majority of mainstream political movements on the left within such regions seem to be geared towards partnerships with the emerging BRIC nations or upon adopting policies that favour a regional response to globalization. That leaves South America again with perhaps the best examples of left nationalism. The left movements of Chávez, Morales, Correa, etc., have all sought to embed forms of nationalization and social protection within the nation-state, while promoting a form of international solidarity between themselves. This has been most notable in the attempts to challenge the extent of foreign direct capital and multinational ownership of the economy, particularly that emanating from the USA.

Like state capitalism, however, the notion of left nationalism has been compromised by the increasing move towards regionalism. As stated, while an analysis of the rise of the left in South America might be divided over whether it seeks to build a pan-national Bolivarian project of mutual forms of progressive nationalism or a more internationalist agenda (Castaneda and Morales 2008), the perception is that the region as a whole is moving towards a single vision of its future development. One can suggest further that if left nationalism is to have a future per se, it might manifest itself at the regional, supranational level. Indeed, one of the often quoted inspirations behind left nationalism – the Austrian Marxist Otto Bauer – has been increasingly used to show how an enlightened national identity might emerge at the supranational or regional level (Roach 2004). Otto Bauer's belief was that nations could be organized not through territoriality but through their personalities or expressions (Bauer 2000). In this way, a national construct can be transformed into a larger regional body that might seek in turn to transform the contemporary state system into entities that can viably contest the common sense of neoliberalism and move towards a post-neoliberal world.

Neoliberalism versus regionalism ?

Rightly or wrongly, the belief that the region is moving to unite in a post-neoliberal polity is something that needs to be taken seriously when looking at the notion that regionalism as a whole might be seen to contest the neoliberal model of economic development. This is indeed something that those who have looked at the emergence of regionalism in global politics have been debating for some time. For some, the development of regionalism has reflected the development of the neoliberal world order and has provided a new mechanism for its governance (Gamble and Payne 1996; Bieler and Morton 2001). Others, however, have suggested that regionalism can manifest itself in new institutional bodies that can regulate the excesses of market rule. Bjorn Hettne, for example, suggests that regionalism can be understood as a form of counter-movement as understood by Karl Polanyi. Regional institutions emerge as bodies that seek to protect citizens from the market anarchy of the global economy. As the welfare state and universal suffrage led to a re-embedding of social relations in the economy during the liberal era, as Polanyi showed, regions have emerged to do likewise during the neoliberal era (Hettne 1994, 2005). Neoliberalism, therefore, will be contested at the regional level, and it is here that future global transformation might take place.

Hettne's observations have been used by others to suggest that as states integrate in greater regional trading blocs, they operate as new forms of social 'filters' whereby regional institutions counter the negative effects of neoliberal globalization through social protection. This is indeed one of the arguments used to analyse the development of the European Union (Wallace 2002; Strange 2006). The idea of a social Europe became synonymous with Jacques Delors and his vision for the future of European integration. In a speech to the British Trade Union Congress (TUC), Delors claimed that the EC would be able to implement labour standards which member states would have to comply with. The speech became almost symbolic in the divisions that it would create between the right and the left over what form regionalism should take. For the neoliberal right, it would underline the potential dangers of the EU, bringing back some of the regulatory principles that it was trying to reform. This was particularly the case in Thatcher's Britain at the time, where the right stressed the dangers of yielding to laws at the regional level which had been removed or reformed at the national level. Paradoxically, it also went some way towards eradicating the idea the left had at that time that European regionalism was effectively developing a 'Europe of the bosses', replacing it with the belief that class struggle could be fashioned at the regional level.

The idea of a social Europe is one that provides a potential site where contestation and transformation of neoliberalism might occur. Here, the argument leads us to suggest that, through regionalism, new forms of politicization can be constructed at the level above the nation-state in order to regulate the excesses of globalization. Yet how much this is a merely European experience is itself another matter for debate. For example, while the Asian crash has led groups such as ASEAN to integrate far more closely than they previously had and move towards a greater formal relationship with Japan and China, many new trends in regionalism have been towards creating greater avenues for free trade. Recent trends within the EU itself have revealed that the potential struggle for a social Europe could be a long-drawn-out one. As many have alluded to, increasingly the EU has marginalized its commitment to social protection in order to pursue greater forms of corporate and market competitiveness (Van Apeldoorn et al. 2008). In light of the euro crisis, the EU's firm measures – its pursuit of austerity measures and cuts in social spending in line with fiscal prudence – have made the case for a social Europe even more remote. Despite this, the structures are in place within the EU as a whole for such a political project to be reinvented, and the idea and relevance of the concept of a social Europe have not in any way diminished in its overall objectives (Strange and Worth 2012).

Interestingly, in South America perhaps the opposite is happening. While there is a very strong idea of regional unity and solidarity in addition to the commitment towards socially protecting the region from the global market, the structures for this to happen are relatively weak. Mercosur,[2] the most recognized form of regional unity, was notorious for its breakdowns in communication, especially between Brazil and Argentina, and is distinctly intergovernmental in its governance. The division between the right and the left has also made it difficult to forge sustainable and successful bodies in which political and economic unity can be built. The US-inspired Free Trade Area of the Americas (FTAA), which was encouraged by the centre-right throughout its genesis in the 1990s, has been criticized by the new left, leading Chávez to create the Bolivarian Alliance for the Americas, which has pledged itself to work towards a common currency and 'reclaiming' the Americas 'back from US imperialism'. The many subregional blocs that have emerged in the continent have been united through the establishment of the Union of South American Nations (Unasur), which includes all states across the region. Unasur appears to model itself on the same directives as those pertaining within the EU, yet with its history of fragmentation ultimate effectiveness remains a long way off.

What seems apparent with the development of regionalism is that as institutional entities these bodies can aid and complement the processes of neoliberalism and can also serve to challenge, contest and check its development. While much work has been done demonstrating that free trade agreements such as NAFTA and FTAA serve to embed neoliberal principles and practices into a wider global market (Rupert 2000), there are other regional bodies that have the capability not just to regulate but also to contest and resist the same principles. It is difficult to foresee what form regionalism will take in the post-crisis era, or whether it can indeed provide a forum wherein neoliberalism can be transformed. If so, it might occur in two different ways. First, regionalism can serve as a basis for a form of progressive politics that could promote some of the democratizing objectives that were outlined in Chapter 3. Alternatively, it can also be used as a mechanism for a renewed form of neo-mercantilism. This does not necessarily entail the doomsday scenario that was depicted by George Orwell in his novel *Nineteen Eighty-Four*, or indeed that imagined by Huntington in his 'clash of civilizations' thesis. However, with the emergence of the so-called BRIC countries, one possible development could be that contender regions base themselves around one specific leader. In Asia the closer integration between ASEAN and China might lead to a wider regional configuration based upon protectionism. Similarly, a like-minded organization might emerge in South Asia, despite interstate antagonism, in which India takes a prominent lead. These would then potentially add to an emerging world of competing regions, with the EU, the post-Soviet 'space' and North and South America all constructing forms of fortresses. The consequences of this could lead to new forms of supranationalism and instabilities which would threaten the current world order.

The potential for regionalism to respond to the neoliberal global market in a supranational neo-mercantilist fashion is also one that needs to be taken with a considerable pinch of salt. Such wider bodies might be popular in regions such as South America, but fail to find favour elsewhere. As argued in Chapter 4, protectionism has only really found great popular support within extreme nationalist discourses which have categorically opposed regional integration. In addition, the sheer number of free trade agreements that have emerged alongside regional blocs makes the emergence of fortress regions unlikely. It is the criss-crossing of horizontal and vertical forms of integration which has led to the term 'open regionalism' (Bersten 1997). Here regional integration is seen as being a series of open agreements whereby free trade is formalized across several organizations with the collective goal of furthering economic cooperation. As a result, rather than constituting stumbling blocks or obstacles to neoliberal development, they very much help to further the process. Certainly, this move has been apparent in the recent developments within regionalism, but the fallout from the financial crisis might provide new alternative initiatives to the sort discussed above.

What type of Prince?

If any of the potential alternatives are to have a realistic chance of challenging the legitimacy of contemporary neoliberalism, they need to forge a movement that seeks to contest its common sense on all fronts. This effectively means not just the combination of a war of position and a war of movement, but the engagement of a wide set of consistent ideas in order to construct an alternative hegemony. This in reality means the construction of a wider coalition across the spectrum of political and civil society. For any of the potential alternatives – 'progressive internationalist', 'national-populist' and 'religious fundamentalism' – to create an effective struggle they need to forge positive cultural, social and political links that popularize their respective objectives so that they can challenge dominant forms of common sense.

For the national-populist challenge to advance its cause it would need to question the very notion of integration by stressing the popular and practical benefits of nationalism and disintegration. At one level, as much nationalist sentiment here is based upon popular and emotional responses, it does have a firm base for this to happen. Yet the lack of support from major political actors and from traditional intellectuals who stress that such positions are dangerous and divisionary make it increasingly difficult for these positions to build wider coalitions. For the religious fundamentalist position to gain momentum, a religious revival is needed globally and regionally in order to challenge the secularization of contemporary global governance. Again, such moves would have to be forged through both the spiritual and the political in order to establish alternative policies and ideologies based upon biblical interpretations. The main obstacles here remain the clash between different religious outlooks. One religious vision would need to become predominant at a global level. As this eventuality is realistically unthinkable then the likely result is either religious conflict, perhaps closer to Huntington's world vision, or a spiritual world based upon separate but compatible religious existence.

From a normative point of view, then, how can a 'progressive internationalist' strategy be built that both establishes a firm alternative based on the premises of social progression and at the same time marginalizes other counter-hegemonic challenges? Or, to borrow from Gramsci, how can it win the 'hearts and minds' of state and civil society (Gramsci 1971). As I hinted earlier, it is not the intention here to add the well-worn 'what is to be done?' to the collection of generalized suggestions/questions made in numerous publications before. Yet I do feel it is useful to stress the need for a political strategy for this to come about. For while ideas and suggestions on how to radically reform the global political economy have emerged from campaigns such as the Tobin tax, the Robin Hood tax, global democratization, a new Bretton Woods system and the establishment of the Bancor, there has to be a major change of direction in the ways in which these suggestions might gain support. These objectives have a chance of being met only through a wide political project that creates a widespread change in the mind-set of civil society. If austerity is still seen as a legitimate tool of action, then the market mind-set has largely emerged unscathed from the crisis. If centre-left political organizations endorse the same position on debt reduction, then any move to challenge this mentality effectively becomes more and more unlikely.

One man who understood the meaning of this form of hegemonic contestation was the British cultural studies pioneer Stuart Hall. Hall's focal point of study was Thatcher's Britain and the growth of Thatcherism in the 1980s. For Hall, Thatcherism was not just a political project or a set of policies grounded in neoliberal ideology, but a sociocultural phenomenon that was geared towards changing the way the public thought about political and economic values. Yet despite this, Thatcherism never managed to win the consent of the 'great majority of the subordinate classes', and in this way it was never hegemonic in the complete sense, but should instead be seen as a hegemonic project (Hall 1988: 91). Hall had argued that, at an earlier point in the 1980s, a fresh project was needed from the left in order to counter the advances made by the right (ibid.: 177–95). The Communist Party magazine in Britain, *Marxism Today*, began to advance such a new project, and *New Times* was the result. This was a project that aimed to construct a new form of political mind-set, seen as one that could contest the market-led policies that were being laid down by Thatcher. *New Times* argued for a post-Fordist form of multiculturalism and post-paternalism which favoured an internationalist or globalist approach in order to face the new realities of production (Hall and Jacques 1989). Yet the reality of the *New Times* project is that it ended by actually establishing the hegemony that Thatcher had attempted to forge a decade earlier.

The real forging of hegemony occurred when left-of-centre parties and organizations accepted general neoliberal principles and, in some cases, contributed to their common sense. No more so was this the case than within Hall's own Britain, where his *New Times* provided the foundations for the 'third way' and subsequently New Labour. Indeed, it was New Labour's own self-styled guru, Peter Mandelson, who claimed that their success would not have been possible without the input of *New Times*. Yet Hall has acknowledged that the New Labour brand merely reinforced and consolidated the neoliberal revolution (Hall 2011). As a result, the left has found it more and more difficult to launch a fresh challenge to the status quo. Perhaps more telling, however, were the criticisms that Hall et al. received when arguing for a new left in the 1980s. For many, the positions proposed seemed too close to the campaigns of Eurocommunism in the 1970s, which were seen as being too conservative, non-radical in outlook and using a distorted interpretation of Gramsci's own work (Harman 1983). These criticisms gain significant credence when observing the emergence of third way 'social democracy' in the 1990s.

For a creditable alternative to emerge from the progressive left requires exactly the sort of unity that Hall suggested. This would require an engagement with Keynesians as well as with the traditional left and with the various progressive strands that were identified in Chapter 3 – a merging of positions and the ability to utilize civil and political partners across the different levels of spatial governance. As neoliberalism is orchestrated through an increasingly uneven collection of state, regional and global forums, then any form of resistance needs to be mobilized to reflect these moves (Shields and Macartney 2011). An alternative should also avoid reverting to some form of 'left nationalism' of the past. It might be that such movements fit into a wider popular-nationalist agenda that forges protectionist measures at either the national or regional level and somehow fuses some of the competing ideologies that were discussed in both Chapters 3 and 4. Here, a common ground might be reached whereby the left and the right can build compatible social strategies and deglobalize the process of neoliberalism through traditional forms of territoriality and nationalism. The battle for hegemony would then once again be waged at the level of the nation-state, with traditional forces of the right and the left re-emerging to determine what form of state entities might develop.

This should be avoided for a number of reasons. First, retreating to policies of the past such as mass nationalization or the traditional planned economy will ultimately fail without these being deployed within a wider global context. The idea of this happening at a supranational or regional level would in the first place be difficult to imagine in some respects (for example, within Europe where divisions exist over European identity) and secondly will only encourage a new fortress mentality. This move would also ultimately run counter to the overall agenda of progressive globalism and would not address the wider problem of global financial governance. More importantly, any attempt at re-establishing forms of national entities, no matter how 'supranational' or 'progressive' they might appear to be, would ultimately create divisions and clashes just as any rivalry of the past did. This brings us back to what Rosa Luxemburg was ultimately referring to a century ago when she wrote about the 'national question' and insisted that any national division would lead to competition, rivalry and prejudice (Luxemburg 1976). As national entities rely upon the idea of some form of 'other' in order to sustain themselves, then divisions are ultimately created that serve to dilute any unified class response to universal change. Gramsci himself was aware of this in examining just how culture and folklore were fused within an emerging Italian consciousness, while Polanyi was at pains to show how humanity's weakness for market rule is often countered by its weakness for nationalism.

More importantly still, if any form of alternative hegemonic strategy is to get off the ground, then the ideological and organizational splits that have dogged such opposition need to be compromised, allowing a wider project. While this will occur, and will generate debate over the form and direction a potential strategy might actually take, the first port of call is to generate the civil and political base for such a challenge. Writing in response to the orthodox positions on strategy at the Second International, Rosa Luxemburg also argued that the finer detail of a revolutionary movement would emerge spontaneously through the process of change (ibid.). This is not to say that challenges to the status quo do not after all need a coherent project of change, but on the contrary that the exact nature of a future order will emerge through a dialectic process which might move far beyond existing social structures. If a truly globalist transformative position is to be sought then its first objective should be to align itself against the common everyday practices of free market economics.

At present, however, unlike those whom he inspired in New Labour, Stuart Hall believes that such a challenge has a long way to go if it is to confront the rhetoric of neoliberalism. Indeed, for Hall, such has been the retreat of socialism and social democracy in the last twenty or thirty years that a renewed challenge appears a distant prospect (Hall 2011). This would also suggest why, in the aftermath of the current financial crisis, the status quo has been allowed to attempt to re-form, amid great unrest and upheaval. Whether a renewal might gain impetus from the many sources of resistance that were discussed in Chapter 3 remains to be seen, but there is a definite need for this to happen in the political arena and for the much-discussed civil resistance to emerge centre stage from the margins. If the austerity measures continue to falter in their current manner, then it seems almost inevitable that a more viable counter-hegemonic coalition will emerge. However, at present Hall's pessimism is understandable.

Conclusion: end of history after all?

This book should perhaps end by revisiting Fukuyama's proclamation of the 'end of history' discussed at the beginning. If I have suggested here that a variety of alternative hegemonic movements have failed to muster a challenge to the neoliberal form of capitalism, then have Fukuyama's arguments in some way been validated? While many forms of opposition have pursued alternatives and highlighted the problems with the post-Cold War order of neoliberalism, they have ultimately failed to challenge its legitimacy. Is it then the case that the power of liberalism is such that it has the capability of dismissing any rival alternatives and carrying on as before, or else reinvents itself in order to address certain concerns that criticisms might have unveiled? As we know, Fukuyama did suggest that certain alternatives would be aired, but that the premise of the free market was too coherent and strong for them (Fukuyama 1992). Likewise, he was at pains to stress that the ascension of liberal capitalism would attract forms of criticism and protest but that ultimately it would be strong enough to fend them off. We could therefore perhaps conclude by arguing that while the arrogant claim that the victory of capitalism had led to an end of history is triumphalist in the extreme, free market capitalism's sustainability is strongly evident.

However, it was precisely the utilization of such a free market liberalism which created the search for alternatives in the first place. The rush towards market rule and the deregulation of finance in the 1990s and 2000s played up to the very notion that, as capitalism had now won its ideological battle against the planned economy, it could now develop without barriers in a truly globalized world. At the same time, discontent over its social Darwinistic character drew criticism and finally succumbed to a crisis of the sort that writers such as Susan Strange had long predicted over a decade earlier (Strange 1997). Such occurrences do not represent a victory of any kind for free market capitalism or suggest that we can proclaim the effective end of any alternative. Indeed, as has been stressed in this book, much of the neoliberal rhetoric has failed. The ability to stimulate growth through market deregulation has failed, leaving the neoliberal model of development practically untenable. The pursuit of austerity has left neoliberalism very much on the defensive and relying upon the conviction that the market might somehow pick itself up and renewal might occur. At this level, one might even argue that neoliberalism is suffering a form of hegemonic or legitimation crisis of the sort that Keynesian political economy suffered in the 1970s. At that time many feared that the return to floating exchange rates and to regional forms of currency stability would lead to a reduction in international economic cooperation. As we have seen in this chapter, many are predicting that a similar pattern could emerge, with the potential of regional groups and the emergence of the BRIC countries creating new spheres of influence.

It is therefore timely for a new alternative hegemonic project to build momentum and to emerge from this period of uncertainty just as the neoliberal project itself did. As I have shown here, there are many forms and types of resistance, which are often difficult to categorize save for their general trajectory. Politically, however, there has been no significant development that suggests that a new order will emerge at the present time, certainly from mainstream 'left' parties, which continue to be directionless in light of the post-Cold War decline of socialism. If the policies of austerity fail to restimulate the market, and if the political landscape fails to add to the critical movements emerging from all forms of social and civil society, then it is not Fukuyama's end of history which will be of significance but Nietzsche's feeble-minded Last Man.

NOTES

1 Introduction

1 Machiavelli wrote *The Prince* in 1513, but it wasn't published until five years after his death, in 1532.

2 Le Pen came third after receiving 17.9 per cent of the vote in the first round.

1 The end of history?

1 Denmark, Sweden and Finland have consistently featured in the top ten of the World Economic Forum's annual 'Global Competitiveness Report' and also appear constantly in the top twenty 'Index of Economic Freedom' list, compiled by the Conservative think tank the Heritage Foundation.

2 Gramsci's *Prison Notebooks* are fragmented and appear disjointed, and parts and subjects within the notes do not follow on from each other as you would expect in a coherent piece. The question of hegemony is one that is central to the notes as a whole, which often look into the cultural and social ways in which it is managed. The best attempt at editing a collection of the *Notebooks* is the Hoare and Nowell-Smith edition (London: Lawrence and Wishart, 1971). Alternatively, a fuller and more authentic translation of the first eight notebooks has been edited and published by Joseph Buttigieg in three volumes (New York: Columbia University Press, 1992; 1996; 2007).

3 For a more detailed account, see part of *Notebook* II (1996) and *Notebook* VIII (2007).

4 For an overview of their 'Statement of Principles', see www.new americancentury.org/statementof principles.htm.

5 Contrast, for example, David Harvey's *The New Imperialism* (2005) with Niall Ferguson's *Colossus* (2004).

2 Resistance and counter-hegemony

1 For examples that incorporate a wide range of positions and ideas, see the edited collections by Gills (2000); Eschle and Maiguashca (2005); and the reader by Amoore (2005). For an excellent critical overview of the literature on resistance and civil society, see Buckley (2013).

2 One of his favourite practices here was to refer to organic intellectuals who contributed to Italian common sense under the title 'Father Bresciani's progeny'. Father Bresciani was a nineteenth-century clergyman and literary figure who wrote fiction from a conservative, anti-nationalist, Catholic viewpoint and focused his work on Sardinian culture (Gramsci 1992, 1996, 2007).

3 Although it should also be stated that, as we have seen in the first chapter, it is those states that have not developed advanced democratic or welfare systems which have been the more extreme in their market approach.

3 Another world is possible?

1 The history of 'micro-nations' dates back to the foundations of the nation-state system, with certain regions claiming to have been excluded from the process of nation-building and arguing their case for independence. The recent increase in this process occurred first in places such as Australia, where an individual who disagreed with

the wheat quotas system initiated by the Western Australian state resulted in him seceding his land from the state. This led to a whole series of copycat successions within the country. The process of secession has spread to other parts of the world with the rise of the Internet and the growth of e-commerce. This has led some to suggest that sovereign states might come under economic stress from such cyber-developments (Ludlow 2001).

2 Its full name being the 'White Overall Movement Building Liberation through Effective Struggle', shortened to 'Wombles' in recognition of a long-running British children's programme where fictional animals cleaned up after humans. One of their activities during the protests would be to hand out leaflets and carry slogans, while dressed as fictitious animals.

3 The veteran singer and aid and debt campaigner Bob Geldof organized the Live Eight concert at Gleneagles in support of debt reduction. He also condemned the protests and actions of 'outsider' groups by arguing that they serve no purpose in pressurizing for international policy on development.

4 Just to clarify, the 'Prince' was used by Machiavelli in the sixteenth century to describe the role modern state leaders should play in establishing their autonomy from the Church. Gramsci referred to the 'modern Prince' throughout his *Prison Notebooks* to illustrate how a socialist/communist party should develop in order to construct its hegemony. Gill's 'postmodern' Prince is geared towards applying this same development to the contemporary era of global politics.

5 The political propaganda played on by the two at the WSF differed. PT and Lula would be presented as revolutionizing the country through grassroots movements. Chávez supporters would simply opt for marches in praise of his name.

6 Post-Soviet states have, with the exception of the various coloured revolutions, often taken distinct top-down governmental approaches that have looked to Moscow as opposed to Brussels for their inspiration. The Communist Party of Russia did attract much interest in the mid-1990s in opposition to the Yeltsin era, but the rise of Putin has sidelined it as an effective party of opposition.

4 Nationalist and exceptionalist responses

1 As an 'All Ireland' political party, Sinn Fein historically regarded itself in a similar role to that of national liberation parties in other parts of the world. Indeed, inspired by James Connolly, it can claim to represent the beginnings of such action. It was keen to operate in the same manner during the Troubles in Northern Ireland. However, as a political party, particularly one operating in a region that has not experienced the same recent conflicts as those in the North, it has had to balance the rhetoric of national liberation with the reactionary and nativist attitudes which, according to accounts, are increasingly prevalent among Sinn Fein voters (O'Malley 2008).

2 For example, the inter-war historian Nesta Webster, who focused on a set of secret organizations, links to communism and the destruction of civilization. She paid particular attention to the idea of the Illuminati and the *Protocols of the Elders of Zion*, which are both used as departure points by contemporary conspiracy theorists.

3 'Good' being those within civil society prepared to stand up to the rules of the 'New World Order' and 'evil' being those elites that are constructing their own impending world government.

4 Perhaps the most bizarre here is from the British author David Icke. According to Icke, prominent global families such as the Dutch and British royal family, the Rothschilds and the Bush and Kennedy families in the USA were all from an alien reptilian-based culture that had been sent to earth to 'rule over human beings'. While Icke, who made his name as a minor sports commentator on the BBC, has been dismissed and ridiculed in his native country, he has gained prominence in parts of North America, Europe and beyond.

5 Perot won a significant 18.9 per cent of the vote in the 1992 election as an independent and 8.4 per cent of the vote in 1996 as the Reform Party candidate. Pat Buchanan could not muster 1 per cent of the overall vote.

6 Effectively, the move to a PR system of voting, which set a minimum representation threshold of 7 per cent, ended liberal and pro-Western parliamentary representation, leaving the CPRF and the LDPR once more as the familiar main focal points of opposition.

7 Pauline Hanson entered the Australian parliament as a member of the Liberal Party, but increasingly incurred the wrath of the party's hierarchy by stating her opposition to globalization and her support for protectionist economics and the restoration of tariffs, as well as her rejection of multiculturalism and her denunciation of immigration. In 1997 she founded the One Nation Party and polled 22 per cent of the vote in the state elections in her native Queensland, and peaked at 9 per cent in the federal elections in 1998. She subsequently lost her seat and the party faded thereafter.

8 Until 2001, the BNP had managed to secure the election of only one short-lived local councillor in East London. Under Griffin's leadership they have managed to get over fifty elected and gain two seats in the European Parliament. Despite this, the party has also become prone to splits in recent years, with several contesting Griffin's leadership or leaving the party. In the local elections of both 2011 and 2012, they imploded somewhat and their number of councillors fell to just three by 2012, prompting some to suggest that they are in terminal decline as an electoral force (Goodwin 2012).

5 The return of God

1 The Buttigieg collection sees his notes on Catholicism scattered across each notebook, from its role within Italian state–Church relations in the first notebook, through to its transnational role in notebook 5, with many entries being under the title 'Catholic Action'. The best-edited selection of Gramsci's work on religion was put together by Derek Boothman in the *Further Selections of the Prison Notebook* (1995), which contained a significant section regarding its role within Gramsci's thought.

2 Wahhabism is the dominant form of Islam within Saudi Arabia, which takes its name from the eighteenth-century Islamic theologian Muhammad ibn Abd al-Whahhab. Salafi or Salafism is the wider term used for it, geared towards the belief that happiness is found through following the traditions and the lifestyles of the prophet Muhammad and the early reproductions of his word (Meijer 2010: 38).

3 Ali Khamenei, who was president from 1981 until Khomeini's death, succeeded him as Supreme Leader.

4 This can be seen in light of the Muslim Brotherhood's election victory in post-Mubarak Egypt in June 2012 and the endorsement of Mohamed Morsi, which has led to several concerns from the West over the future direction of the country.

5 Current estimates put the

number of Pentecostals at the end of the twentieth century in excess of 150 million, with those taking on evangelical characteristics numbering up to 400 million (Lechner and Boli 2005: 173).

6 The age of austerity

1 Alan Greenspan held the position from 1987 until 2006.

2 In the same way that Gramsci became very interested in the manner in which popular working-class publications became so influential in developing a consciousness of common sense in Italy in the early part of the twentieth century, he would have been fascinated by the 'tabloid culture' of the popular press that has been especially influential in Anglophone states. Cable TV networks such as Fox News and tabloid print newspapers have become key outlets in communicating the popular 'common sense' of the 'working' and 'ordinary' citizen.

3 According to Gallup's study, non-Hispanic black supporters make up 6 per cent, as opposed to the 13 per cent proportion in the population at large. A similar disparity is seen in income, where 19 per cent of their supporters earn less than $30,000 per annum as opposed to 25 per cent in the population at large.

4 Tobin's own suggested rate for the currency transaction tax was around 0.5 per cent, while others in Attac (the international movement working towards 'social, environmental and democratic alternatives in the globalisation process') have suggested that it could be levied at 1 per cent. Sarkozy's proposed rate was 0.1 per cent.

7 Neoliberalism and potential transformation

1 The idea of 'import substitution' was favoured by dependency theorists and those who followed the Singer-Prebisch thesis, whereby, in order to address the trading discrepancy that emerged from developing states gaining less from importing manufacturing and technological goods from the developed world in exchange for primary products, domestic manufacturing markets are developed in order to lower imports.

2 Mercosur is made up of Brazil, Argentina, Uruguay and Paraguay, with Venezuela waiting for its final ratification process to be realized.

BIBLIOGRAPHY

Adib-Moghaddam, A. (2007) 'Manufacturing war: Iran in the neo-conservative imagination', *Third World Quarterly*, 28(3): 635–53.

Al-Nabhani, T. (1995) *The Islamic State*, London: al-Khilafah Publications.

— (1996) *Economic System of Islam*, London: al-Khilafah Publications.

Amoore, L. (2005) *The Global Resistance Reader*, London: Routledge.

Anderson, B. (1991) *Imagined Communities*, London: Verso.

Anti-Fascist Forum (2001) *My Enemy's Enemy*, Montreal: Kersplebedeb.

Archibugi, D. (ed.) (2003) *Debating Cosmopolitanism*, London: Verso.

Archibugi, D. and D. Held (eds) (1995) *Cosmopolitan Democracy: An Agenda for a New World Order*, Cambridge: Polity.

Augelli, E. and C. Murphy (1988) *America's Quest for Supremacy and the Third Word: A Gramscian Analysis*, London: Pinter.

Barber, B. (1996) *Jihad vs McWorld*, New York: Ballantine.

— (2004) *Fear's Empire: War, Terrorism and Democracy*, New York: Norton.

Bartholomeusz, T. and C. de Silva (eds) (1998) *Buddhist Fundamentalism and Minority Identities in Sri Lanka*, Albany: State University of New York Press.

Bauer, O. (2000) *The Question of Nationalities and Social Democracy*, Minneapolis: University of Minnesota Press.

Beasley-Murray, J., M. Cameron and E. Hershberg (2009) 'Latin America's left-turn: an introduction', *Third World Quarterly*, 30(2): 319–30.

Beeson, M. (2009) 'Hegemonic transition in East Asia? The dynamics of Chinese and American power', *Review of International Studies*, 35(1): 95–112.

— (2010) 'The Washington Consensus vs state capitalism', in M. Beeson and N. Bisley, *Issues in 21st Century World Politics*, Basingstoke: Palgrave.

Berglund, H. (2011) 'Hindu nationalism and gender: a challenge to the Indian women's movement', *International Feminist Journal of Politics*, 13(1): 83–99.

Bersten, F. (1997) 'Open regionalism', *World Economy*, 20(5): 545–65.

Betz, H.-G. (1994) *Radical Right Wing Populism in Western Europe*, New York: St Martin's Press.

Bhagwati, J. (2004) *In Defense of Globalization*, Oxford: Oxford University Press.

Biagiotti, I. (2004) 'The World Social Forums: a paradoxical application of participatory democracy', *International Social Science Journal*, 56(4): 529–40.

Bieler, A. and A. Morton (eds) (2001) *Social Forces in the Making of the New Europe*, Basingstoke: Palgrave.

Billings, D. (1990) 'Religion as opposition: a Gramscian analysis', *American Journal of Sociology*, 96(1): 1–31.

Birchfield, V. (2005) 'Jose Bove and the globalisation counter-movement in France: a Polanyian interpretation', *Review of International Studies*, 31(3): 581–98.

Birchfield, V. and A. Freyberg-Inan (2004) 'Constructing opposition in the age of globalization: the potential of ATTAC', *Globalizations*, 2(1): 278–304.

BNP (British National Party) (2001) *General Election Manifesto*, www.bnp.org.uk/policies/2001_manifesto.htm.

Brassett, J. (2010) *Cosmopolitanism and Global Financial Reform: A Pragmatic Approach to the Tobin Tax*, London: Routledge.

Buchanan, P. (1998) 'Free trade is not free', Address to the Chicago Council on Foreign Relations, 18 November.

Buckley, K. (2013) *Global Civil Society and Transversal: The Globalisation–Contestation Nexus*, London: Routledge.

Bukharin, N. (1925) *Historical Materialism*, New York: International Publishers.

Burawoy, M. (2003) 'For a sociological Marxism: the complementary convergence of Antonio Gramsci and Karl Polanyi', *Politics and Society*, 31(2): 193–261.

Burbach, R. (2001) *Globalization and Post-Modern Politics*, London: Pluto.

Butko, T. (2004) 'Revelation and revolution: a Gramscian approach to the rise of political Islam', *British Journal of Middle Eastern Studies*, 31(1): 41–62.

Calhoun, C. (1997) *Nationalism*, Buckingham: Open University Press.

Callinicos, A. (2003) *An Anti-Capitalist Manifesto*, Cambridge: Polity.

— (2009) *Imperialism and Global Political Economy*, Cambridge: Polity.

Camilleri, J. and J. Falk (1992) *The End of Sovereignty*, London: Edward Elgar.

Cardoso, H. (2001) *Charting a New Course: The Politics of Globalisation and Social Transformation*, Lanham, MD: Rowman & Littlefield.

Carter, E. (2005) *The Extreme Right in Western Europe: Success or Failure?*, Manchester: Manchester University Press.

Castaneda, J. (2006) 'Latin America's left turn', *Foreign Affairs*, 85(3): 28–43.

Castaneda, J. and M. Morales (eds) (2008) *Leftovers: Tales of the Latin American Left*, London: Routledge.

Castells, M. (1997) *The Power of Identity*, Oxford: Blackwell.

Cerny, P. (1997) 'Paradoxes of the competition state: the dynamics of political globalization', *Government and Opposition*, 32: 251–67.

Chakrabortty, A. (2012) 'Economics has failed us: but where are the fresh voices?', *Guardian*, 16 April.

Chandler, D. (2004) *Constructing Global Civil Society*, London: Palgrave.

— (2007) 'Hollow hegemony: theorising the shift from interest-based to value-based international policy making', *Millennium: Journal of International Studies*, 35(3): 703–23.

Chase-Dunn, C. and E. Reese (2007) 'The World Social Forum: a global party in the making?', in K. Sehm-Patomaki and M. Ulvila, *Global Political Parties*, London: Zed Books, pp. 53–92.

Chin, C and J. Mittelman (2000) 'Conceptualising resistance to globalization', in B. Gills (ed.), *Globalization and the Politics of Resistance*, Basingstoke: Palgrave, pp. 29–47.

Choate, P. (2010) 'Two views of the Tea Party appeal', NPR, 6 February.

Chomsky, N. (1996) *Manufacturing Consent: Noam Chomsky and the Media*, ed. M. Achbar, Montreal: Black Rose.

— (2007) *What We Say Goes: Conversations on US Power in a Changing World*, London: Hamish Hamilton.

Christian Coalition (2012) 'About us', www.cc.org/about_us.

Clift, B. (2003) *French Socialism in a Global Era: The Political Economy of the New Social Democracy in France*, London: Continuum.

Cohen, S. (2000) *Failed Crusades: America and the Tragedy of Post-Communist Russia*, New York: Norton.

Cox, M. (2004) 'Empire, imperialism and the Bush doctrine', *Review of International Studies*, 30(4): 585–608.

Cox, M. and P. Shearman (2000) 'After the fall: national extremism in post-communist Russia', in P. Hainsworth (ed.), *The Politics of the Extreme Right: From the Mainstream to the Margins*, London: Pinter, pp. 224–47.

Cox, R. (1987) *Power, Production and World Order: Social Forces in the Making of History*, New York: Columbia University Press.

— (1996) *Approaches to World Order*, Cambridge: Cambridge University Press.

Crouch, C. (2011) *The Strange Non-Death of Neoliberalism*, Cambridge: Polity.

Croucher, S. (2004) *Globalization and Belonging: The Politics of Identity in a Changing World*, Lanham, MD: Rowman & Littlefield.

Cuninghame, P. and C. Ballesteros Corona (1998) 'A rainbow at midnight: Zapatistas and autonomy', *Capital and Class*, 66: 12–23.

Dahrendorf, R. (1990) *Reflections on the Revolution in Europe*, New York: Times Books.

Dale, G. (ed.) (2011) *First the Transition then the Crash: Eastern Europe in the 2000s*, London: Pluto.

David, H. (2007) 'Transnational advocacy in the eighteenth century: transatlantic activism and the anti-slavery movement', *Global Networks*, 7(3): 367–82.

Debord, G. (2002) *Guy Debord and the Situationist International*, ed. T. McDonough, Cambridge, MA: MIT Press.

Delors, J. (1988) Speech to the British Trade Union Congress.

Døving, C. (2010) 'Anti-Semitism and Islamophobia: a comparison of imposed group identities', *Tidsskrift for Islamforskning – Islam og minoriteter*, 2: 52–76.

Downes, G. (2009) 'China and India: the new powerhouses of the semi-periphery?', in O. Worth and P. Moore (eds), *Globalization and the 'New' Semi-Peripheries*, Basingstoke: Palgrave, pp. 114–35.

Drainville, A. (2004) *Contesting Globalization: Space and Place in the World Economy*, London: Palgrave.

Dunphy, R. (2004) *Contesting Capitalism? Left Parties and European Integration*, Manchester: Manchester University Press.

Eatwell, R. and M. Goodwin (2010) *The New Extremism in 21st Century Britain*, London: Routledge.

Elliott, L. (2012) 'Too much austerity will be damaging, IMF reports', *Guardian*, 17 April.

Enloe, C. (1996) 'Margins, silences and bottom rungs: how to overcome the underestimation of power in the study of international relations', in S. Smith, K. Booth and M. Zalewski (eds), *International Theory: Positivism and Beyond*, Cambridge: Cambridge University Press, pp. 186–203.

Eschle, C. and B. Maiguashca (eds) (2005) *Critical Theories, International Relations and the Anti-Globalisation Movement: The politics of global resistance*, London: Routledge.

Evans, T. (2011) 'The limits of tolerance: Islam as counter-hegemony', *Review in International Studies*, 37(4): 1751–73.

Ferguson, N. (2004) *Colossus*, London: Gardners.

Fisher, W. and T. Ponniah (eds) (2003) *Another World is Possible: Popular Alternatives to Globalization at the World Social Forum*, London: Zed Books.

Foucault, M. (1998 [1979]) *A History of Sexuality: An Introduction*, London: Vintage.

— (2008) *The Birth of Biopolitics: Lectures at the College 1978–1979*, Basingstoke: Palgrave.

Frank, A.-G. (1966) 'The development of under-development', *Monthly Review*, 18(4): 17–37.

Freyberg Inan, A. and V. Birchfield (2004) 'Constructing opposition in the age of globalization: the potential of ATTAC', *Globalizations*, 1(2): 278–304.

Friedman, T. (2005) *The World is Flat: A Brief History of the Twenty-first Century*, New York: Farrar, Straus and Giroux.

Fukuyama, F. (1989) 'End of history', *National Interest*, 16: 3–18.

— (1992) *The End of History and the Last Man*, London: Penguin.

— (2012) 'The future of history: can liberal democracy survive the decline of the middle class', *Foreign Affairs*, 91(1): 53–61.

Gall, G. (2009) 'In search of a Scottish outside left', in M. Perryman (ed.), *Breaking Up Britain: Four Nations after a Union*, London: Lawrence & Wishart, pp. 159–72.

Gallup (2010) 'Tea Parties are fairly mainstream in their demographics', www.gallup.com/poll/127181/tea-partiers-fairly-mainstream-demographics.aspx.

Gamble, A. (2009) *The Spectre at the Feast*, Basingstoke: Palgrave.

Gamble, A. and A. Payne (1996) *Regionalism and World Order*, Basingstoke: Palgrave.

Germain, R. (2010) *Global Politics and Financial Governance*, Basingstoke: Palgrave.

Germain, R. and M. Kenny (1998) 'Engaging Gramsci: International Relations theory and the new Gramscians', *Review of International Studies*, 24(1): 3–21.

Giddens, A. (1998) *The Third Way*, Cambridge: Polity.

Gill, S. (2000) 'Towards a post-modern prince? The battle in Seattle as a moment in the new politics of globalisation', *Millennium: Journal of International Studies*, 29(1): 131–40.

Gills, B. (ed.) (2000) *Globalization and the Politics of Resistance*, Basingstoke: Palgrave.

Githens-Mazer, J. (2010) 'Mobilization, recruitment, violence and the street: radical violant *takfiri* Islamism in early twenty-first-century Britain', in R. Eatwell and M. Goodwin, *The New Extremism in 21st Century Britain*, London: Routledge.

Goodwin, M. (2011) *New British Fascism: The Rise of the British National Party*, London: Routledge.

— (2012) 'The BNP is finished as an electoral force', *Guardian*, 4 May.

Gramsci, A. (1971) *Selections from the Prison Notebooks*, London: Lawrence & Wishart.

— (1992) *Antonio Gramsci – Prison Notebooks*, vol. 1, New York: Columbia University Press.

— (1995) *Further Selections from the Prison Notebooks*, Minneapolis: University of Minnesota Press.

— (1996) *Antonio Gramsci – Prison Notebooks*, vol. 2, New York: Columbia University Press.

— (2007) *Antonio Gramsci – Prison Notebooks*, vol. 3, New York: Columbia University Press.

Grandin, G. (2006) *Empire's Workshop: Latin America, the United States and the Rise of the New Imperialism*, New York: Metropolitan Books.

Griffin, N. (2002) 'Cults, jets and greed: the frantic rush to "One World"', www.bnp.org.uk/articles/rush_globalism.htm.

Grugel, J. and P. Riggirozzi (2012) 'Post-neoliberalism in Latin America: rebuilding and reclaiming the state after crisis', *Development and Change*, 43(1): 1–21.

Hainsworth, P. (2008) *The Extreme Right in Western Europe*, London: Routledge.

Hall, P. and D. Soskice (2001) *Varieties of Capitalism: The Institutional Foundations of Comparative*

Advantage, Oxford: Oxford University Press.

Hall, S. (1988) *The Hard Road to Renewal*, London: Verso.

— (1996) *Stuart Hall: Critical Dialogues in Cultural Studies*, London: Routledge.

— (2011) 'The neoliberal revolution', *Soundings*, 48: 9–28.

Hall, S. and M. Jacques (ed.) (1989) *New Times: Changing Face of Politics in the 1990s*, London: Lawrence & Wishart.

Hall, S. and T. Jefferson (eds) (1993) *Resistance through Rituals: Youth subcultures in post-war Britain*, London: Routledge.

Halliday, F. (1999) 'Islamophobia reconsidered', *Ethnic and Racial Studies*, 22(5): 892–902.

Hann, C. and K. Hart (eds) (2009) *Market and Society: The Great Transformation Today*, Cambridge: Cambridge University Press.

Hannon, E. (2010) 'Does India still need a Hindu Nationalist Party', *Foreign Affairs*, www.foreignpolicy.com/articles/2010/04/30/does_india_still_need_a_hindu_nationalist_party.

Hardt, M. and A. Negri (2000) *Empire*, Harvard, MA: Harvard University Press.

Harman, C. (1983) 'Gramsci versus reformism', Pamphlet, Socialist Workers Party, London.

Harten, S. (2011) *The Rise of Evo Morales and the MAS*, London: Zed Books.

Harvey, D. (2003) *The New Imperialism*, Oxford: Oxford University Press.

— (2005) *A Brief History of Neoliberalism*, Oxford: Oxford University Press.

— (2010) 'Crisis of capitalism', Talk given to the Royal Society of Arts, 26 April.

— (2010) *The Enigma of Capital*, Oxford: Oxford University Press.

Hayek, F. (1931) *Prices and Production*, New York: Augustus M. Kelly.

— (2001 [1944]) *The Road to Serfdom*, London: Routledge.

Haynes, J. (2007) *Religion and Development: Conflict or Cooperation?*, London: Palgrave.

Helbawy, K. (2010) 'The Muslim Brotherhood in Egypt: historical evolution and future prospects', in K. Hroub, *Political Islam: Content versus Ideology*, London: Saqi, pp. 61–86.

Held, D. and D. Kaya (2007) *Global Inequality: Patterns and Trends*, Cambridge: Polity.

Held, D. and A. McGrew (2003) *The Global Transformation Reader*, Cambridge: Polity.

— (2007) *Globalization/Anti-Globalization*, 2nd edn, Cambridge: Polity.

Herman, E. and N. Chomsky (1998) *Manufacturing Consent: The Political Economy of the Mass Media*, New York: Pantheon Books.

Herman, E. and R. McChesney (1997) *The Global Media: The New Missionaries of Global Capitalism*, London: Castell.

Hettne, B. (1994) 'The regional factor in the formation of a new world order', in Y. Sakamoto (ed.), *Global Transformation: Challenges to the State-System*, Tokyo: United Nations University Press.

— (2005) 'Beyond the new regionalism', *New Political Economy*, 10(4): 543–71.

Hilley, J. (2001) *Malaysia: Mahathirism, Hegemony and the New Opposition*, London: Zed Books.

Hirst, P. and G. Thompson (1996) *Globalization in Question*, Cambridge: Polity.

Hitler, A. (1992) *Mein Kampf*, London: Pimlico.

Holloway, J. (2002) *Change the World without Taking Power: The Meaning of Revolution Today*, London: Pluto.

Huntington, S. (1996) *The Clash of Civilisations and the Remaking of World Order*, New York: Simon & Schuster.

Ignazi, P. (2003) *Extreme Right Parties in Western Europe*, Oxford: Oxford University Press.

Jenkins, P. (2002) *The Next Christendom: The Coming of Global Christianity*, Oxford: Oxford University Press.

John Birch Society (2000) 'Get the US out of the UN', www.jbs.org/.

Joseph, J. (2002) *Hegemony: A Realist Analysis*, London: Routledge.

Kaldor, M. (2003) *Global Civil Society: An Answer to War*, Cambridge: Polity.

Keddie, N. (2003) *Modern Iran: Roots and Results of Revolution*, New Haven, CT: Yale University Press.

Keohane, R. (1984) *After Hegemony*, New York: Princeton University Press.

Kepel, G. (1994) *The Revenge of God: The Resurgence of Islam, Christianity and Judaism in the Modern World*, Cambridge: Polity.

— (2006) *The Trail of Political Islam*, 4th edn, London: I.B. Tauris.

Keynes, J.-M. (1942a) 'On commodity control', in *Activities 1940–46. Shaping the Post-War World: and Commodities, Collected Writings of John Maynard Keynes*, vol. XXVII, Cambridge: Cambridge University Press.

— (1942b) 'The international regulation of primary products', in *Activities 1940–46. Shaping the Post-War World: Employment and Commodities, Collected Writings of John Maynard Keynes*, vol. XXVII, Cambridge: Cambridge University Press.

— (2004) *The End of Laissez-Faire*, New York: Prometheus Books.

Kindleberger, C. (1981) 'Dominance and leadership in the international economy', *International Studies Quarterly*, 25(2): 242–54.

Klein, N. (2002) *Fences and Windows: Dispatches for the front lines of the globalization debate*, London: HarperCollins.

— 'More democracy – not more political strongmen', *Guardian*, 3 February 2003, at http://www.globalpolicy.org/ngos/advocacy/conf/2003/0203klein.htm

Krauthammer, C. (2004) 'In defence of democratic realism', *National Interest*, 77: 15–25.

Krugman, P. (1999) 'Enemies of the WTO', *Slate*, 23 November.

— (2012) 'Nobody understands debt', *New York Times*, 1 January.

Laclau, E. and C. Mouffe (1985) *Hegemony and Socialist Strategy*, London: Verso.

Lane, D. (1996) *The Rise and Fall of State Socialism*, Cambridge: Polity.

Laqueur, W. (1996) *Fascism: Past, Present, Future*, Oxford: Oxford University Press.

Lechner, F. and J. Boli (2005) *World Culture: Origins and Consequences*, Oxford: Blackwell.

Leite, J.-C. (2005) *The World Social Forum: Strategies of Resistance*, Chicago, IL: Haymarket.

Lipset, S. and S. Rokkan (eds) (1967) *Party Systems and Voter Alignments: Cross National Perspectives*, New York: Free Press.

Ludlow, P. (ed.) (2001) *Crypto Anarchy, Cyberstates and Pirate Utopias*, Cambridge, MA: MIT Press.

Luxemburg, R. (1976) *The National Question*, New York: Monthly Review Press.

Macartney, H. (2011) 'Crisis for the state or crisis of the state?', *Political Quarterly*, 82(2): 193–203.

Machiavelli, N. (1984) *The Prince*, London: Penguin.

Mandaville, P. (2007) *Global Political Islam*, London: Routledge.

Markotich, S. (2000) 'Serbia: extremism from the top and a blurring of right into left', in P. Hainsworth (ed.), *The Politics of the Extreme Right: From the Mainstream to the Margins*, London: Pinter, pp. 268–87.

Marsden, L. (2008) *For God's Sake: US Foreign Policy and the Christian Right*, London: Zed Books.

Marx, K. (1967) *The Eighteenth Brumaire*

of Louis Bonaparte, Moscow: Progress Press.

— (1976) *Capital*, vol. 1, London: Penguin.

— (1993) *Grundrisse*, London: Penguin.

Mayer, N. (2004) 'Nouvelle judéophobie ou vieil antisémitisme?', *Raisons politiques*, 16: 91–103.

Mazaar, M. (2003) 'George W. Bush, idealist', *International Affairs*, 79(3): 503–22.

McLeod, D. and N. Lustig (2011) 'Inequality and poverty under Latin America's new left regimes', Tulane Economics Working Paper Series 1117.

Mearsheimer, J. (1990) 'Back to the future: instability in Europe after the Cold War', *International Security*, 15(1): 5–56.

Meijer, R. (2010) 'Salafism: doctrine, diversity and practice', in K. Hroub, *Political Islam: Content versus Ideology*, London: Saqi, pp. 37–61.

Mudde, C. (2007) *Populist Radical Right Parties in Europe*, Cambridge: Cambridge University Press.

Mudde, C. and J. van Holsteyn (2000) 'The Netherlands: explaining the limited success of the extreme right', in P. Hainsworth (ed.), *The Politics of the Extreme Right: From the Mainstream to the Margins*, London: Pinter, pp. 144–71.

Munck R. (1986) *The Difficult Dialogue: Marxism and Nationalism*, London: Zed Books.

— (2007) *Globalization and Contestation: The new great counter-movement*, London: Routledge.

— (2010) 'Marxism and nationalism in the era of globalization', *Capital and Class*, 34(1): 45–53.

Murray, K. (2012) 'Christian "Renewalism" and the production of free market hegemony', *International Politics*, 49(2): 260–76.

Murray, K. and O. Worth (2012) 'Building consent: hegemony, "conceptions of the world" and the role of evangelicals in global politics', *Political Studies*, forthcoming, published online: doi: 10.1111/j.1467-9248.2012.01003.x.

Nairn, T. (2005) *Faces of Nationalism: Janus Revisited*, 2nd edn, London: Verso.

Nanda, M. (2010) *The God Market: How globalization is making India more Hindu*, Delhi: Random House.

Nederveen-Pieterse, J. (2004) *Globalisation and Culture: Global Melange*, Lanham, MD: Rowman & Littlefield.

Nesvetailova, A. (2007) *Fragile Finance: Debt, Speculation and Crisis in the Age of Global Credit*, Basingstoke: Palgrave.

Nietzsche, F. (2006) *Thus Spoke Zarathustra*, Cambridge: Cambridge University Press.

Nimni, E. (1985) 'Great historical failures: Marxist theories of nationalism', *Capital and Class*, 25.

OECD (2011) 'Income distribution and poverty in OECD countries', Paris: OECD.

O'Malley, E. (2008) 'Why is there no radical right party in Ireland?', *West European Politics*, 31(5): 960–77.

Panizza, F. (2005) 'Unarmed utopia revisited: the resurgence of left-of-centre politics in Latin America', *Political Studies*, 53(4): 716–34.

Patriot Action (2011) www.patriotaction-network.com/.

Paul, R. (2008) *The Revolution: A Manifesto*, New York: Grand Central Publishing.

— (2009) *End the Fed*, New York: Grand Central Publishing.

Peck, J. (2010) *Constructions of Neoliberal Reason*, Oxford: Oxford University Press.

Petras, J. (2007) *Rulers and Ruled in the US Empire: Bankers, Zionists, Militants*, Atlanta, GA: Clarity Press.

Phillips, M. (2005) *Londonistan: How*

Britain Is Creating a Terror State Within, New York: Encounter Books.

Picciotto, S (1991) 'The internationalisation of the state', *Capital and Class*, 15(1): 43–63.

Polanyi, K. (2001 [1944]) *The Great Transformation: The Political and Economic Origins of Our Time*, Boston, MA: Beacon Press.

— (1968) *Primitive, Archaic and Modern Economies: Essays of Karl Polanyi*, ed. G. Dalton, New York: Anchor Books.

Prasad, M. (2006) *The Politics of Free Markets: The Rise of Neoliberal Economic Policies in Britain, France, Germany and the United States*, Chicago, IL: Chicago University Press.

Putin, V. (2001) 'Russia at the turn of the millennium', *Current Politics and Economics of Russia, Eastern and Central Europe*, 15(3): 241–53.

Radice, H. (2000) 'Responses to globalisation: a critique of progressive nationalism', *New Political Economy*, 5(1): 5–21.

Roach, S. (2004) 'Minority rights and the dialectic of the nation: Otto Bauer's theory of the nation and its contributions to multicultural theory and globalization', *Human Rights Review*, 6(1): 91–105.

Robertson, P. (1991) *The New World Order*, Dallas, TX: Word.

Robinson, N. (2012) 'The edges of Europe, the "Eastern Marches" and the problematic nature of a "wider Europe"', in G. Strange and O. Worth, *European Regionalism and the Left*, Manchester: Manchester University Press.

Ross, M. (1999) 'The political economy of the resource curse', *World Politics*, 51(2): 297–322.

Rothbard, M. (1994) *The Case against the Fed*, Auburn, AL: Ludwig von Mises Institute.

Rupert, M. (2000) *Ideologies of Globalization*, London: Routledge.

— (2009) 'Imperial consent and post-Fordist militarism in the USA', *Globalizations*, 6(1): 121–5.

Ryan, B. and O. Worth (2010) 'On the contemporary relevance of left nationalism', *Capital and Class*, 34(1): 54–9.

Sachs, J. (2005) *The End of Poverty: Economic Possibilities for Our Time*, London: Penguin.

Saikal, A. (2004) *Modern Afghanistan: A History of Struggle and Survival*, London: I.B. Tauris.

Sanbonmatsu, J. (2003) *The Postmodern Prince: Critical Theory, Left Strategy and the Making of a New Political Subject*, New York: Monthly Review Press.

Schumacher, E. F. (1943) 'Multilateral clearing', *Economica*, 10: 150–65.

Seligson, M. (2006) 'The rise of populism and the left in Latin America', *Journal of Democracy*, 18(3): 81–95.

Seliktar, O. (2000) *Failing the Crystal Ball Test: The Carter Administration and the Fundamentalist*, Westport, CT: Praeger.

Sheridan, L. (2006) 'Islamophobia pre and post September 11th, 2001', *Journal of Interpersonal Violence*, 21: 317–36.

Shields, S. and H. Macartney (2011) 'Space, the latest frontier? A scalar-relational approach to critical IPE', in S. Shields, I. Bruff and H. Macartney (eds), *Critical International Political Economy: Dialogue, Debate and Dissensus*, Basingstoke: Palgrave, pp. 27–42.

Shields, S., I. Bruff and H. Macartney (eds), *Critical International Political Economy: Dialogue, Debate and Dissensus*, Basingstoke: Palgrave.

Shipman, A. (2002) *The Globalization Myth: Why the protestors have got it wrong*, Cambridge: Icon Books.

Shirk, S. (2004) *How China Opened Its Door*, Washington, DC: Brookings Institution.

Shnirelman, V. (1998) 'Russian neo-pagan myths and anti-Semitism', International Centre for the Study of Anti-Semitism, Hebrew University, Jerusalem.

Skidelsky, R. (2009) *Keynes: The Return of the Master*, London: Allen Lane.

Smith, A. (1995) *Nations and Nationalism in a Global Era*, Cambridge: Polity.

Sousa Santos, B. de (2006) *The Rise of the Global Left: The World Social Forum and Beyond*, London: Zed Books.

Stanley, L. (2011) 'Does crisis matter? Everyday experience and resistance during the global financial crisis', Paper for presentation at the ECPR General Conference, Reykjavik.

Steger, M. (2005) *Globalism: Market Ideology meet Terrorism*, Lanham, MD: Rowman & Littlefield.

Stiglitz, J. (2006) *Making Globalization Work*, New York: W. W. Norton.

Strange, G. (2006) 'The left against Europe: a critical engagement with new constitutionalism and structural dependency theory', *Government and Opposition*, 41(2): 197–229.

— (2011) 'China's post-Listian rise: beyond radical globalisation theory and the political economy of neoliberalism', *New Political Economy*, 16(5): 539–59.

Strange, G. and O. Worth (2012) *European Regionalism and the Left*, Manchester: Manchester University Press.

Strange, S. (1997) *Casino Capitalism*, Manchester: Manchester University Press.

Sundaram, V. (2006) 'Impact of globalisation on Indian culture', Bolo, www.boloji.com/index.cfm?md=Content&sd=Articles&ArticleID=2458.

Taguieff, P.-A. (1994) *Sur la Nouvelle droite: jalons d'une analyse critique*, Paris: Descartes et Cie.

Tannsjo, T. (2008) *Global Democracy: The Case for a World Government*, Edinburgh: Edinburgh University Press.

Tea Party (2011) www.teaparty.org/about.php.

TerraViva (2007) 'News from World Social Forum 2007', Nairobi: World Social Forum.

Thatcher, M. (2002) *Statecraft*, London: HarperCollins.

Thomas, S. (2005) *The Global Resurgence of Religion and the Transformation of International Relations*, Basingstoke: Palgrave Macmillan.

Torbjörn, T. (2010) *Global Democracy: The Case for a World Government*, Edinburgh: Edinburgh University Press.

Turner, J. (2012) 'The rise of Salafi jihadism: challenges to the status quo global order and the role of U.S. hegemony', Doctoral thesis, University of Surrey.

Van Apeldoorn, B., L. Drahokoupil and L. Horn (eds) (2008) *Contradictions and Limits of Neoliberal European Governance – from Lisbon to Lisbon*, Basingstoke: Palgrave.

Van der Pijl, K. (1998) *Transnational Classes and International Relations*, London: Routledge.

Verkhovsky, A. (2000) 'Ultra nationalists in Russia at the onset of Putin's rule', *Nationalities Papers: The Journal of Nationalism and Ethnicity*, 28(4): 707–22.

Von Mises, L. (1934 [1912]) *The Theory of Money and Credit*, London: Jonathan Cape.

— (1949) *Human Action: A Treatise on Economics*, New York: Yale University Press.

Wagner, D. (1998) 'Evangelicals and Israel: theological roots of a political alliance', *Christian Century*, 4 November, pp. 1020–26.

Walker, R. (1994) 'Social movements/world politics', *Millennium: Journal of International Studies*, 23(3): 669–700.

Wallace, H. (2002) 'Europeanisation and globalisation: complementary or contradictory trends', in S. Breslin, C. Hughes, N. Phillips and B. Rosamond (eds), *New Regionalism in the Global Political Economy: Theories and Cases*, London: Routledge.

Waltz, K. (1993) 'The new world order', *Millennium: Journal of International Studies*, 22(2): 187–95.

Watson, I. (2002) 'Rethinking resistance: contesting neoliberal globalisation and the Zapatistas as a critical social movement', in J. Abbott and O. Worth, *Critical Perspectives on International Political Economy*, Basingstoke: Palgrave, pp. 108–39.

Williamson, J. (1989) 'What Washington means by policy reform', in J. Williamson (ed.), *Latin American Readjustment: How Much Has Happened*, Washington, DC: Institute for International Economics.

Witherell, W. (1995) 'The OECD multilateral agreement on investment', *Multinational Corporations*, 4(2): 1–14.

Wolf, M. (2004) *Why Globalization Works*, New York: Yale University Press.

Worth, O. (2002) 'The Janus-like character of counter-hegemony: progressive and nationalist responses to globalisation', *Global Society*, 16(3): 297–315.

— (2005) *Hegemony, International Political Economy and Post-Communist Russia*, Aldershot: Ashgate.

— (2008) 'The poverty and potential of Gramscian thought in international relations', *International Politics*, 45(6): 633–49.

— (2009) 'Unravelling the Putin myth: strong or weak Caesar?', *Politics*, 29(1): 53–61.

— (2012) 'Beyond the Third Way: regionalism and socialist renewal in Europe', in G. Strange and O. Worth, *European Regionalism and the Left*, Manchester: Manchester University Press.

— (2013) 'Polanyi's *magnum opus*? Assessing the application of the counter-movement in International Political Economy', *International History Review*, 35(3).

Worth, O. and J. Abbott (2006) 'Land of (false) hope?: the contradictions of British opposition to globalisation', *Globalizations*, 3(1): 49–63.

Worth, O. and K. Buckley (2009) 'The World Social Forum: "post-modern prince or court jester?"', *Third World Quarterly*, 30(4): 641–61.

Worth, O. and C. Kuhling (2004) 'Counter-hegemony, anti-globalisation and culture in International Political Economy', *Capital and Class*, 84: 31–43.

Worth, O. and P. Moore (eds) (2009) *Globalization and the 'New' Semi-Peripheries*, Basingstoke: Palgrave.

WSF (World Social Forum) (2007) 'Charter of Principles of the World Social Forum: Nairobi', São Paulo: WSF.

Xiaochuan, Z. (2002) 'Reform the international monetary system', *BIS Review*, Basle: Bank for International Settlements.

Zapatistas (1998) *Zapatista Encuentro: Documents from the First Intercontinental Encounter for Humanity and against Neoliberalism*, New York: Seven Stories Press.

Zaslove, A. (2008) 'Exclusion, community, and a populist political economy: the radical right as an anti-globalization movement', *Comparative European Politics*, 6(2): 169–89.

INDEX